Drive-Ins of New Mexico

Michael Kilgore

Published in the United States

ISBN: 978-1-7333655-9-8

Library of Congress Control Number: 2023903992

First printing: March 2023

Table of Contents

Table of Contents v

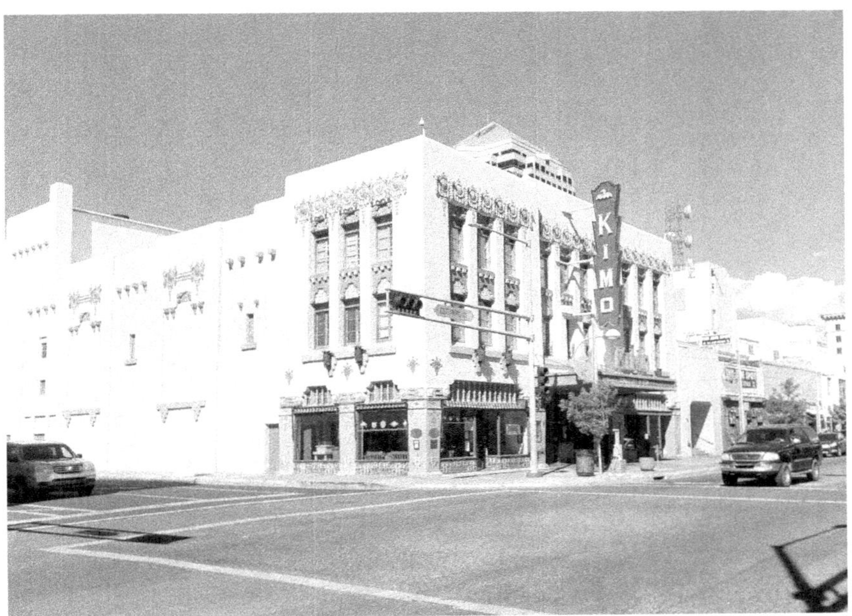

It's not a drive-in, but the Kimo Theatre in Albuquerque is always worth a mention. It's been around since 1927, and its Pueblo Deco architecture is gorgeous. I wish we had more movie palaces like this. Definitely worth a visit! 2019 photo by the author.

South Las Vegas, August 1960

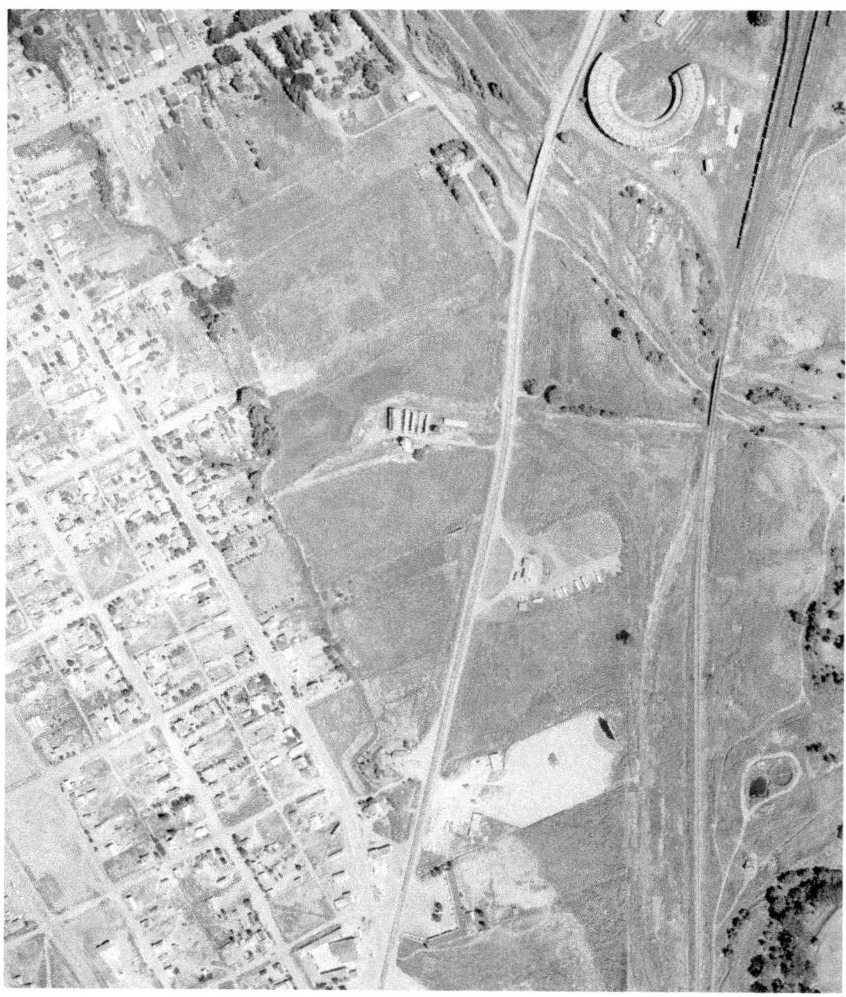

I can't say enough nice things about the New Mexico Department of Transportation. Solving the mystery of the second Vegas Drive-In (see Page 97), they sent me this aerial of the south side of Las Vegas. Thanks to the landmark of the old railway roundhouse (that U-shaped building, still there today), I know exactly where this short-lived ozoner once operated.

Introduction

This book is an experiment.

It's the third of a series, following *Drive-Ins of Colorado* and the enhanced section edition of *Drive-Ins of Route 66*. (Fourth if you count the rushed, less accurate first edition of the Route 66 book, but I'd prefer to forget about that one.)

Those earlier books were designed with a fun magazine style, with lots of illustrations and a layout that curled the text around them. Their electronic versions were either a page-by-page image of the print book or an uneven flowing adaptation with some badly enlarged photos interrupting the text. *Drive-Ins of New Mexico* is designed to be an electronic book first, more easily read on smartphones and simpler text readers such as the Kindle Paperwhite.

(Having said that, as I prepared a physical version, I couldn't help adding a few graphics to assist and entertain you, the print reader. Actually quite a few.)

At some point I also need to mention that I'm only going to cover the state's drive-in theaters that opened by 2020. The very newest drive-ins are mostly (solely?) inspired by the Covid pandemic, so it's hard for me to tell how to document their stories.

Another big advantage is that this type of book should be easier to update. Because something in this book is wrong, I'm sure of it. There are so many details about so many drive-ins that more of them surface as the months go by, and some of them run counter to what we thought we knew. Corrections and additions are a lot easier to handle for an e-book than a paperback. (In fact, corrections and bonus content are available at Carload.com under Books / New Mexico.)

What you've got is incomplete. It will always be incomplete, because there will always be details that we just don't have. It's still the very best information about the state's many drive-in theaters.

If you have a relative with a photo album from the time he worked at the drive-in, or if your local library has back issues of a newspaper I couldn't get to, and you can add more information to this collection of drive-in histories, please drop me a line at mkilgore@carload.com.

Thanks for reading. I hope you enjoy this.

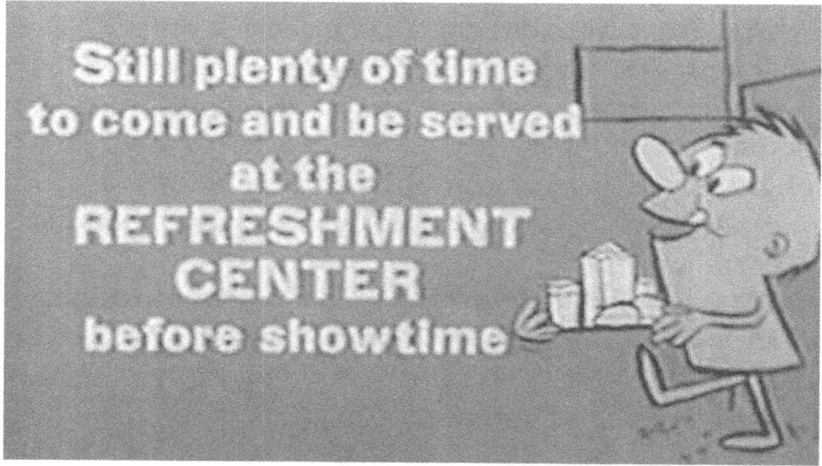

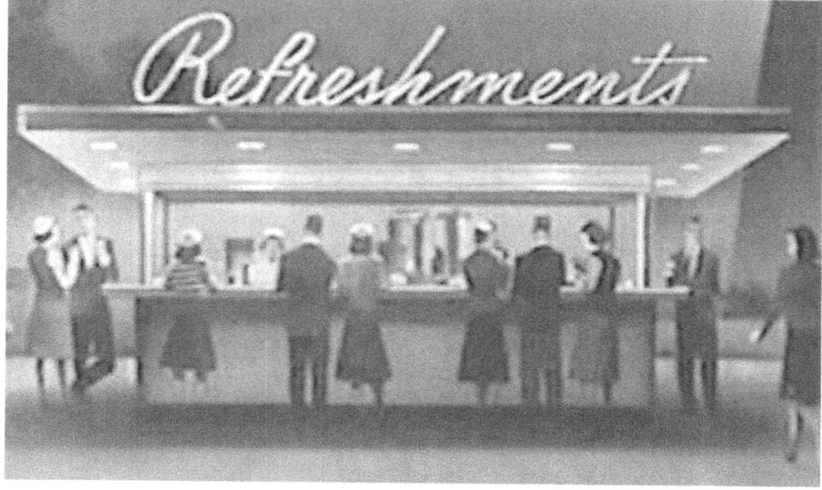

A Brief History of Drive-Ins

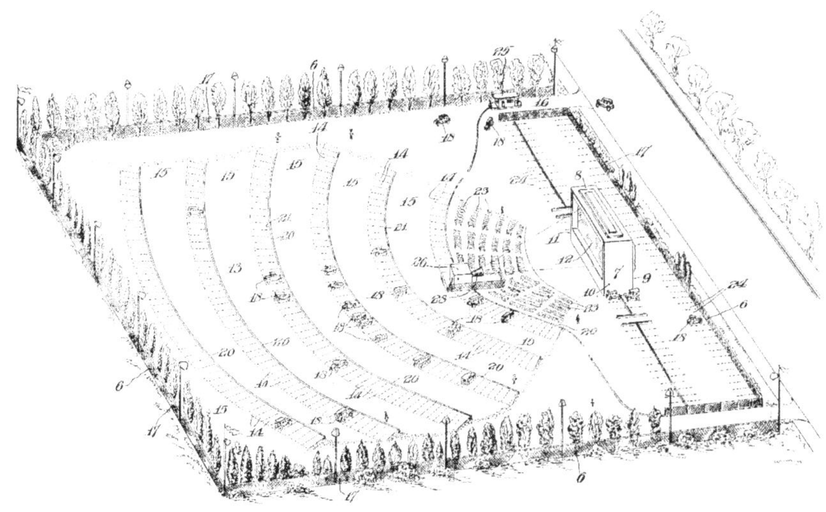

One of the drawings from Richard Hollingshead Jr.'s original drive-in theater patent.

Although silent-movie "drive-ins" had previously popped up now and then, (see Las Cruces, for example), their history really starts with inventor Richard Hollingshead Jr., who got the first drive-in theater patent on June 1, 1933. What he really invented wasn't the outdoor theater — it was the drive-in ramp, which angled each car up to point at the screen. You might also give him credit for most viewing fields' clamshell design.

The Shaky Start

Hollingshead's first location, which opened June 6, 1933, near Camden NJ, was not a success. It was popular

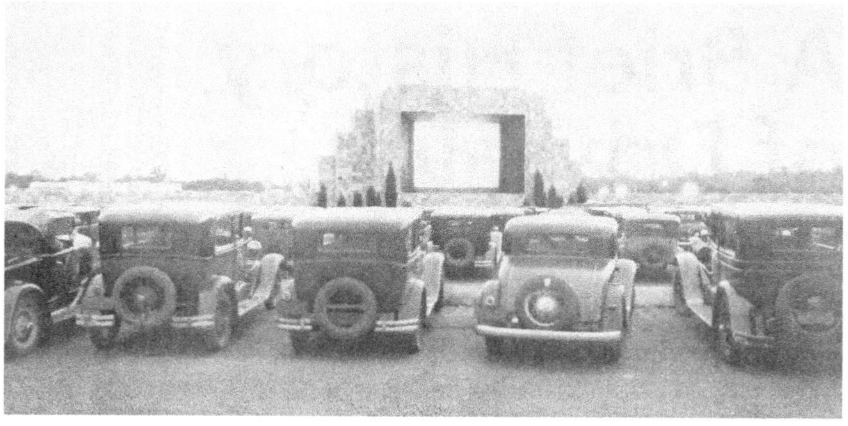

A front-seat view of the first drive-in theater in Camden NJ, as it appeared in *Motion Picture Herald*.

enough, but as with most 1930s drive-ins, its main problem was sound — no one had invented in-car speakers. Loudspeakers supplied the sound to the drive-in's patrons and often beyond, to its annoyed neighbors. An equally serious problem was content — distributors weren't eager to rent films for it. Decades later, Hollingshead told the *Philadelphia Inquirer* that one of his first rentals "was three years old and cost us $400 for four days. The last time the film had run was in a little (theater) that paid $20 a week for it." He sold the Camden drive-in theater within three years to an indoor theater owner, with better film connections, who moved it to Union NJ.

The Hollingshead patent didn't fare much better, as most competitors built similar sites without paying royalties. But potential drive-in builders weren't sure they could safely ignore the patent. That uncertainty, along with the early sound problems, kept the drive-in business from growing quickly. Fewer than two dozen permanent drive-in theaters were built in the first five years, often using naming alternatives such as "motor-in" or "outdoor theatre." Some small-town entrepreneurs operated short-lived versions using little more than bedsheets, loud-

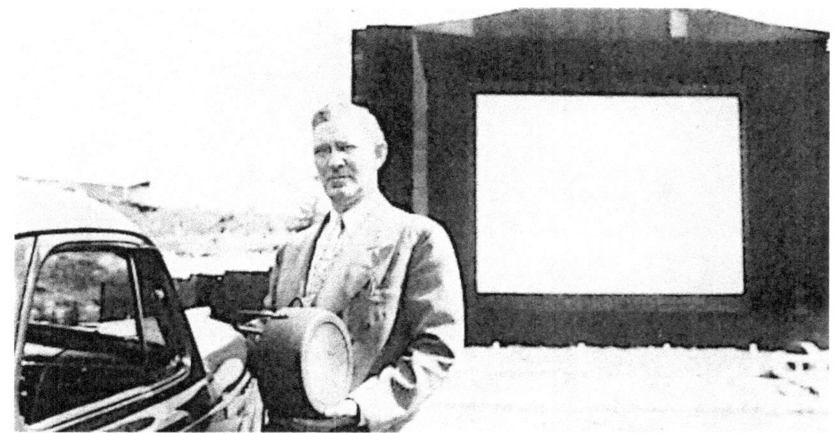

An early advancement in sound came in 1940 in Providence RI. That city's drive-in added in-car amplifiers, which attendants attached each night. The installation for 550 cars cost $10,000, or about $200,000 in today's dollars. In this photo from *The Exhibitor*, manager Walter D. McGhee shows off one of the eight-inch devices.

speakers, and film projectors. When the *Film Daily Year Book* published the first national drive-in theater list in 1942, it could find only 95 of them.

The Postwar Explosion

After World War II ended, American soldiers returned home ready to start families and enjoy some entertainment. For most, their choices were live performance, radio, or the movies. Television was only available in some of the big cities, and it was really expensive. A typical 1951 set cost over $2500 in today's dollars and could receive just three black and white broadcasts on a screen smaller than today's computer monitors. The only way to watch a movie was to see whatever was showing, a current film or a reissue, at a theater.

So in the early postwar years, every factor lined up in favor of drive-ins. Car ownership in the US rose by over

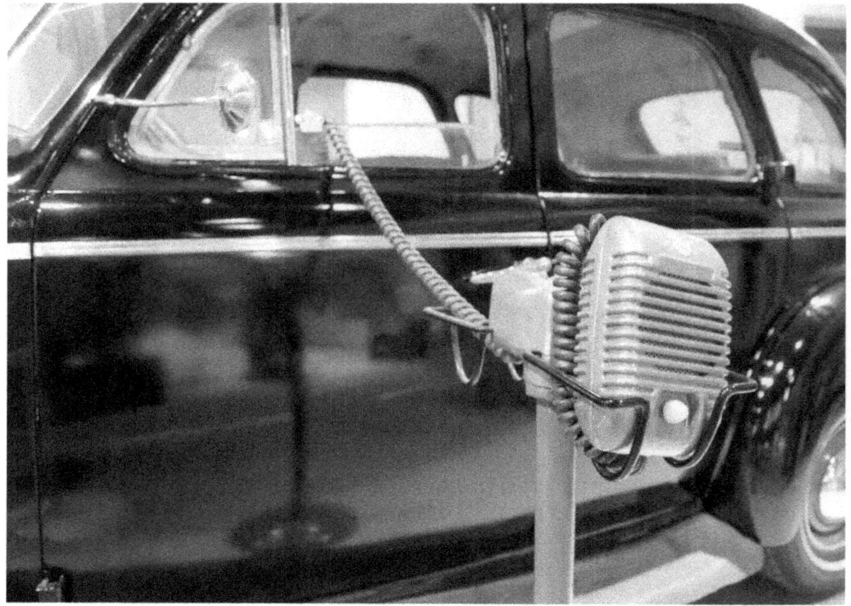

One factor that accelerated the drive-in boom was the post-war availability of the inexpensive in-car speaker. Its classic shape symbolized the drive-in age. 2019 photo by the author at the National Route 66 Museum in Elk City OK.

65% between 1945 and 1951. The rapidly growing population increasingly moved to suburbs and away from traditional downtown theaters. Indoor theaters also required parking, which could be difficult or expensive, patrons were expected to dress up, and families with children needed to find babysitters.

Outdoor movies had none of those drawbacks. Patrons were urged to "come as you are" and bring the kids along. Daylight-saving time wasn't widespread yet, so drive-ins could start at a decent hour. Hollywood slowly switched to movies in color, even as it continued to create films suitable for the whole family. Plentiful cheap land at the edge of town beckoned developers. The drive-in became a fun new place for families to visit.

The number of drive-ins grew steadily, but the real explosion came after October 1949 when the US Supreme

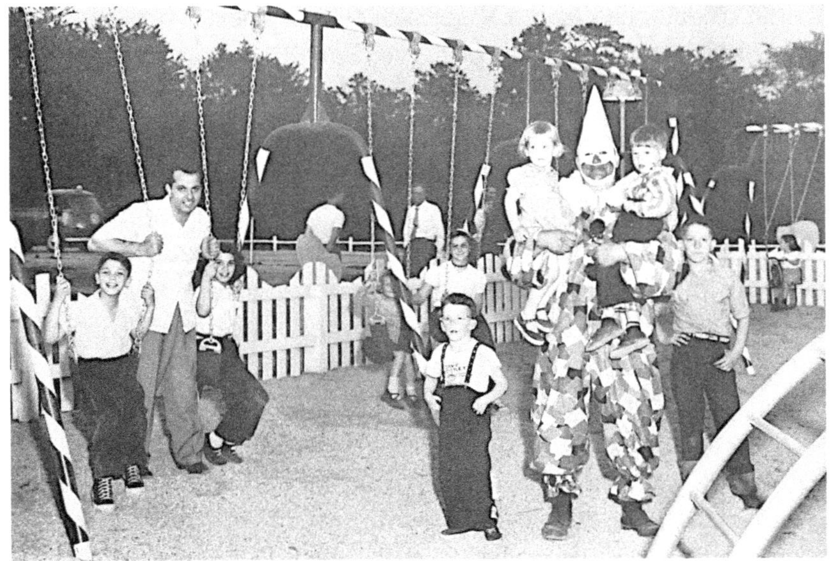

Drive-in theaters built increasingly elaborate playgrounds, which drew children, who brought their parents along. They were often monitored by attendants, such as the clown shown above at Long Island NY's Bayshore-Sunrise Drive-In, which also had a motor-driven Ferris wheel. Photo from the 1955-56 *Theatre Catalog*.

Court ruled, in effect, that Hollingshead's ramp could not be patented. In one year, the number of US drive-ins more than doubled, from about 750 in 1949 to over 1700 in 1950. That number would have grown even higher, but in September 1950, as the Korean War flared, the US National Production Authority began requiring its approval to use certain building materials for entertainment facilities. Despite that speed bump, drive-in construction resumed normally within a couple of years, and the drive-in population grew to over 4300 by 1955.

The Long Decline

After 1955, the number of US drive-ins leveled out for the next decade. Then most of the factors that led to their growth peeled away one by one. Television expanded to almost every city, and TV set prices dropped from unthinkable to merely expensive. Families snapped them up; 83 percent of American homes had TV in 1958, up from a mere 9 percent in 1950.

At all theaters, fewer films worked for the whole family; most explored more mature topics, and some were too childish for grown-ups to enjoy. Casual wear became acceptable at indoor theaters, and there were more of them close to suburban homes as part of new shopping centers. National adoption of daylight-saving time in 1967 sliced a crucial hour off already limited drive-in schedules.

Movie-viewing at home became more convenient. Home Box Office launched in 1972, the first of a wave of commercial-free, uncut movie channels for home viewing. Perhaps the final, most lethal drive-in killer was the video cassette recorder. As VCRs dropped in price in the 1980s, video rental stores popped up. A family could line up a

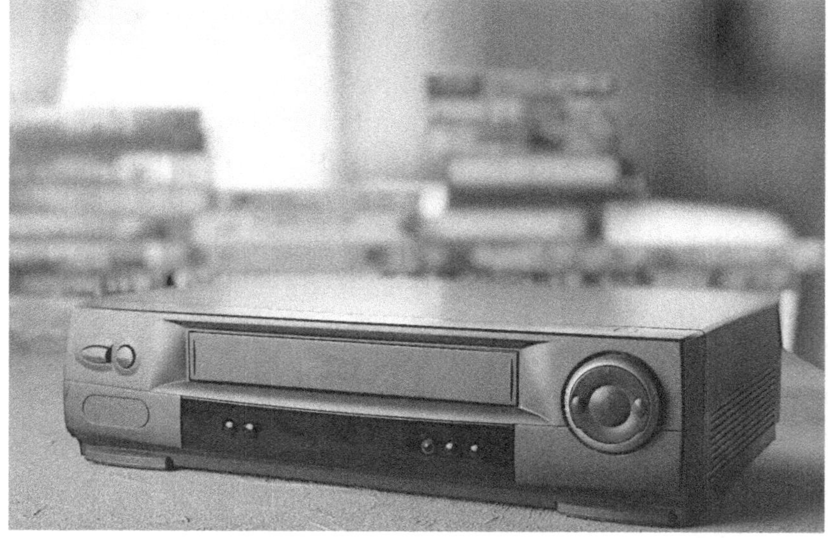

Possibly the greatest single factor in the death of so many drive-ins was the arrival of the video cassette recorder (VCR). Few drive-ins survived the 1980s, the decade when VCRs became common in homes. Photo © olegkrugllyak / Depositphotos.com.

double- or triple-feature with homemade snacks for less than the cost of a night out.

Many drive-ins reacted by trying to provide viewers with an experience they couldn't get on television. In the mid-1950s, that meant wide-screen movies, and most pre-existing drive-ins added wings to their screens. Westerns and other family fare faded. As the typical car became less likely to include children, drive-in movie-makers shifted their attention to teenagers and young adults. In the 1960s and 1970s, that often meant horror or titillation films, which were eventually labeled as R-rated. Some drive-ins went even further, showing softcore sexy R movies or even hardcore adult films.

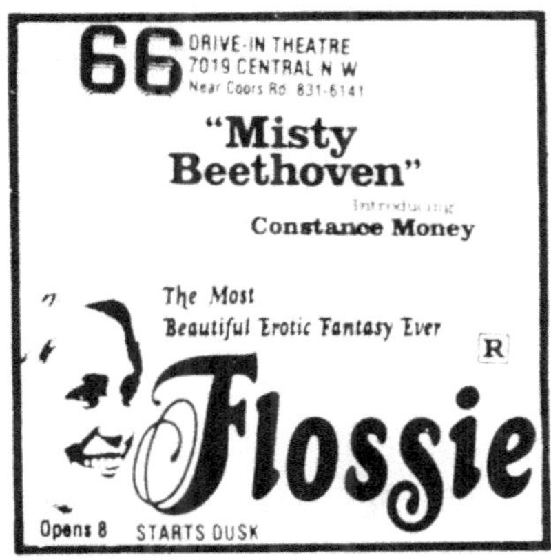

Albuquerque's 66 Drive-In turned to sexier films in its later years, running afoul of the city zoning code restricting the locations of "adult entertainment establishments." The 66 was accused of mislabeling X-rated movies as R. Is that what was going on in this 1980 ad from the *Albuquerque Tribune*?

As cities and suburbs expanded, they often encircled previously remote drive-ins. When a developer wanted a contiguous piece of land for a shopping mall or a housing tract, he could offer to buy a drive-in. Some landowners had figured this out decades earlier, offering short-term leases to drive-in theaters while planning to cash out once their parcels became valuable. Combine that with the dwindling crowds and neighborhood pressure against X-rated movies, selling out was often the landowner's best choice.

21st Century Rediscovery

Most drive-ins that persisted past the year 2000 were either popular in small but not tiny towns (about 5,000-10,000 people), or were in metropolitan areas stuck on parcels of land that were unappealing for other uses. For the survivors, a few new factors tilted back in their direction.

Disney had always produced family-friendly movies, and it kick-started a modern-day trend with Best Picture nominee *Beauty and the Beast* (1991). Hoping for similar success, other filmmakers returned to making animated movies that the whole family could enjoy. Studios expanded production of comic book adaptations and other

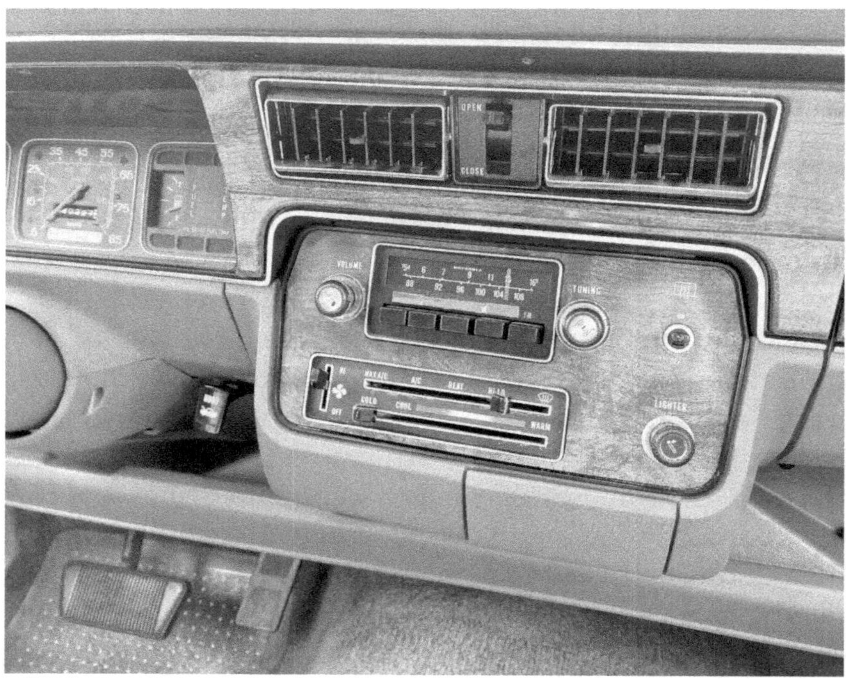

When most cars included FM radios, that allowed drive-in operators to switch to less expensive FM radio sound. Photo of a 1982 AMC station wagon by Christopher Ziemnowicz.

cartoonish action movies, so drive-ins once again had a product to sell to both children and their parents.

The FM radio transmitter supplemented and often replaced window-hanging speakers since most cars now had FM stereo radios. Patrons enjoyed richer movie audio than they had from the tinny window-hanging speakers, and drive-in owners didn't have to maintain and replace them every month.

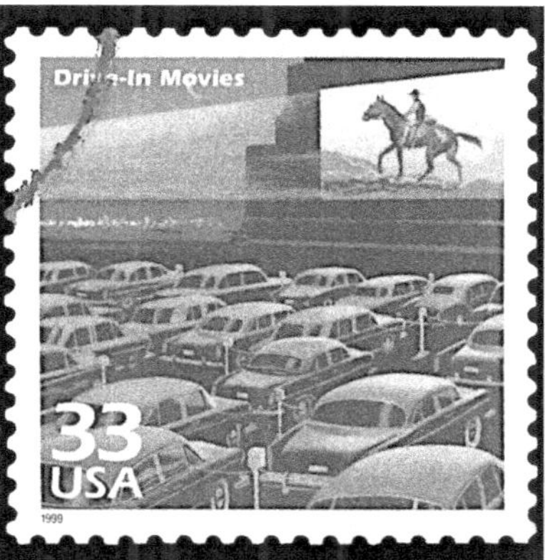

The USPS issued a drive-in theater stamp in 1999 as part of its "Celebrate the Century" set. It was one of 16 representing the 1950s. Photo © Mmphotos2017 / Dreamstime.com.

Near the close of the last century, when the US Postal Service asked its users to vote on the topic that best commemorated the 1950s, they were surprised that the big winner was drive-in movies. Postwar baby boomer children had become parents themselves and grew nostalgic for the advantages and fun of the drive-in. Surviving drive-ins showed an uptick in attendance around the turn of the century.

But that didn't mean they were out of the woods. Almost no new drive-ins were being built, and every year, a few drive-ins closed as their aging owner-managers cashed out, retired, or both.

Drive-In Economics

Let me pause for a moment to describe a typical drive-in theater's sources of income. In the early days, drive-ins often rented or even purchased films and kept the ticket proceeds. In 1954, concession stand sales accounted for just 22% of the average drive-in's income. Those days are long gone. Today, a very high percentage of each ticket goes to the movie's distributor, so modern drive-ins make most of their money through the concession stand.

In effect, most drive-in theaters operate as seasonal outdoor restaurants with an entertainment theme. They're popular and a lot more fun, but keeping that in mind, you can see how it's hard to get rich running a drive-in. It also explains why some drive-in owners get really cheesed when patrons bring in their own food. The best drive-ins sell food so good that you'd look forward to choosing it for dinner. Even for the bad ones, I still make a point to buy popcorn and soda, a drive-in's most profitable products. But I have digressed long enough. Back to history.

The Digital Imperative

Theatrical digital movie projection, using hard drives instead of reels of film, was first demonstrated in 1999. After 15 years of tweaking the format and planning a new distribution system, Hollywood decided to switch. The word came down from studios that they would no longer spend $5 million or more per movie to print a limited number of copies on fragile, heavy film. They required all theaters to convert to digital projection so they could use easier-to-ship, reusable hard drives instead.

Drive-ins always needed powerful film projectors to show films. Their larger screens sat farther away than indoor theaters', and ambient city light interfered more than a darkened room. To comply with Hollywood's demand, they needed special, expensive digital projectors. As I just mentioned, drive-ins typically don't clear a ton of money, so many of them feared that they'd have to close when the last film versions of movies disappeared.

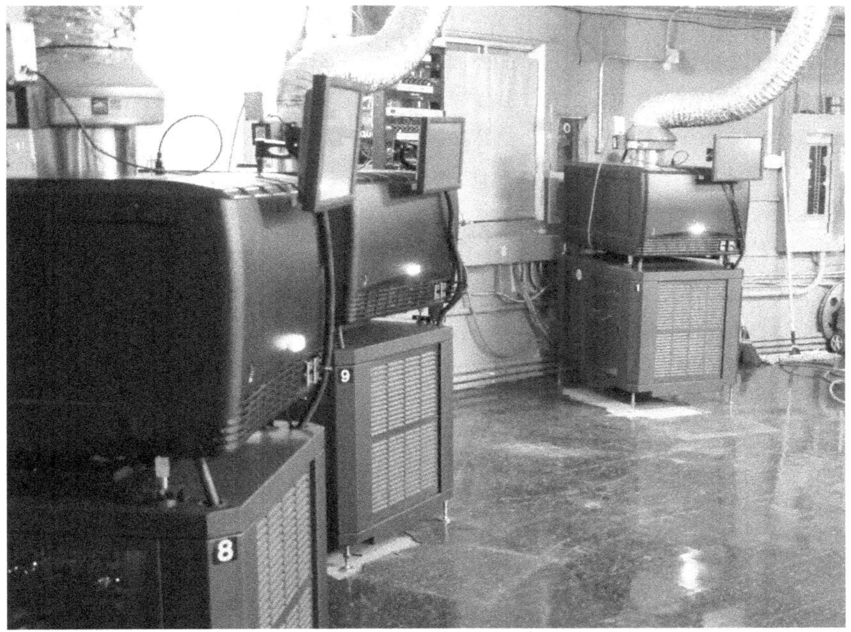

If buying a single drive-in digital projector is expensive, imagine laying out the cash for nine of them. Here are three of the Glendale (AZ) 9 Drive-In's new projectors. 2013 photo by the author.

In 2013, Honda spotlighted these owners' plight through Project Drive-In, where fans could vote for their favorite theater. Honda awarded projectors to nine winners, and the contest drew public attention to the drive-ins that didn't win.

When the final wave of digital conversion hit soon after, some drive-ins shut down, but not as many as some had feared. And here's the thing — those that survived found that whatever hadn't killed them made them stronger.

The digital system has its benefits. Picture quality is always excellent. "Prints" of any movie are more easily available. Drive-in screens can show broadcast sports or huge video games. And having invested all that money in equipment, today's drive-ins have a stronger incentive to stay open year after year. Brand-new drive-ins are being built, and new-wave "pop-up" boutique drive-ins thrive in converted parking lots. During the Covid pandemic, more people came to appreciate the natural social distancing and excellent ventilation that drive-ins offer.

The steady pressure of rising land value continues to close a few drive-ins every year. But some of the original attractions of a drive-in are now causing about as many to pop up in their place. Substitute FM radio sound for a loudspeaker and once again, all a theatrical entrepreneur really needs is a projector, a screen, and a parking lot.

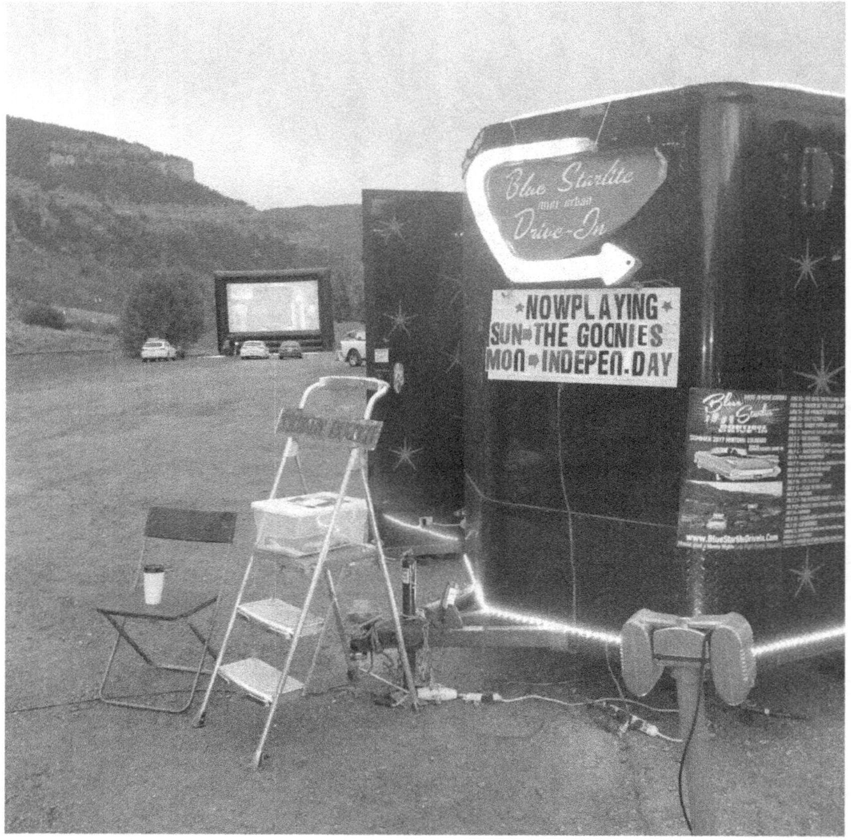

The Blue Starlite Mini Urban (sic) Drive-In Theater operated for several summers in Minturn CO. (These days, they stick close to the Austin TX area.) Wherever it sets up, it's a great example of the new style of pop-up drive-in. 2017 photo by the author.

New Mexico's 82 Drive-Ins

ordered by Opening Date

Oct. 13, 1946 – Drive-In, Hatch

Sept. 26, 1947 – Cactus, Albuquerque

July 1948 – Yucca, Clovis
Aug. 10, 1948 – Fiesta, Carlsbad
Aug. 20, 1948 – Organ / Fiesta, Las Cruces
Oct. 29, 1948 – County / No Name, Tucumcari

March? 1949 – Sunset / Star-Lite, Socorro
May 5, 1949 – Sky-Vu, Hobbs
May 18, 1949 – Starlite, Roswell
June 15, 1949 – 85, Raton

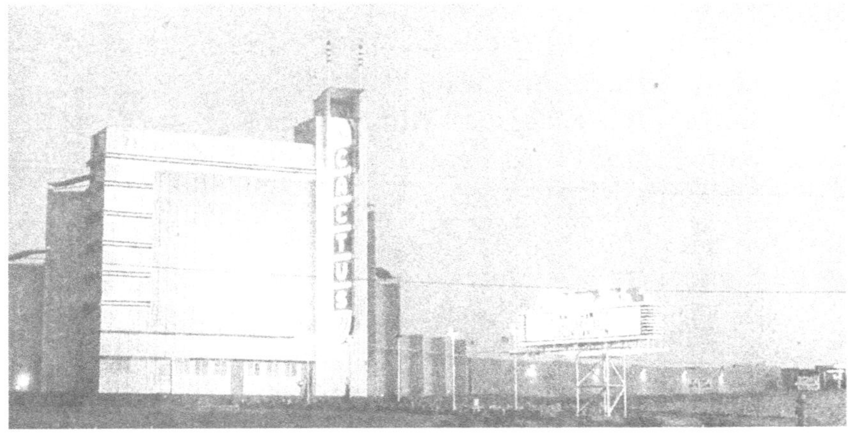

The Cactus was the first large drive-in in the state. Photo from the Feb. 14, 1948 issue of *Motion Picture Herald*.

July 27, 1949 – Star / Linda Vista / Northside,
Albuquerque
    Aug. 7, 1949 – Tesuque, Albuquerque
    Aug. 30, 1949 – 66, Albuquerque
    Dec. 9, 1949 – Starlite, Alamogordo

    April 9, 1950 – Circle B, Artesia
    April 9, 1950 – Varsity, Portales
    April 28, 1950 – Chico / Starlighter, Española
    April? 1950 – Vegas, Las Vegas
    May 12, 1950 – Four Lane, Clovis
    May 30, 1950 – Mesa, Farmington
    June 9, 1950 – Pueblo, Tesuque
    July 1950 – Mt. Vue, Ruidoso
    July 4, 1950 – Yucca, Santa Fe
    Aug. 8, 1950 – Eagle, Hobbs

    April 20, 1951 – Canal, Tucumcari
    July 12, 1951 – Palms / Jet / Palms, Williamsburg
    July 27, 1951 – Ballojak, Roswell
    July 31, 1951 – Jingle Bob, Roswell
    August? 1951 – Copper / Sundowner, Arenas Valley
    Sept. 21, 1951 – Yucca, Lovington
    Sept. 28, 1951 – Yucca, Gallup
    Oct. 10, 1951 – Mimbres, Deming
    Oct. 18, 1951 – Terrace, Albuquerque
    Nov. 28, 1951 – Sunset, Albuquerque
    November? 1951 – Zia, Belen

    January? 1952 – Star, Eunice
    April 13, 1952 – Corral, Carlsbad
    April 24, 1952 – Sierra / Sierra Vista, Socorro
    May 29, 1952 – Apache, Farmington
    June? 1952 – Panther, Jal
    June? 1952 – Trail, Clayton

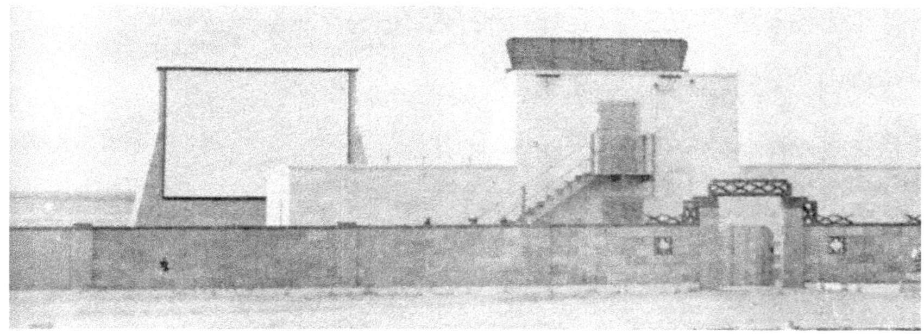

The *Albuquerque Progress*, published by Albuquerque National
Bank, included this photo of the freshly built Duke City Drive-In.

July 4, 1952 – La Fonda, Clovis
July 20, 1952 – Rocket, Las Cruces
Aug. 15, 1952 – Sky-Ranch, Santa Rosa
November? 1952 – Coyote, Tatum

Feb. 17, 1953 – Duke City, Albuquerque
Sept. 9, 1953 – Wildcat, Lovington
1953? – Trade Wind, Hobbs
1953? – Crawley's, Portales
1953? – Silver Sky-Vue, Silver City

Feb. 2, 1954 – Yucca, Alamogordo
Feb. 23, 1954 – San Jose / Tri-C / Route 25,
Albuquerque
March? 1954 – Trails, Milan
April? 1954 – Joy, Anthony
April 17, 1954 – Chief, Lordsburg
June 1, 1954 – Rincon, Aztec
Aug. 6, 1954 – Hollywood, Ruidoso
Aug. 11, 1954 – Valley, Farmington
December? 1954 – Chief, Shiprock
1954 – Sunset, Hobbs

March 5, 1955 – Jet / Route 54, Tularosa

Aug. 4, 1955 – Hermosa, Artesia
Nov. 24, 1955 – Flamingo Twin, Hobbs

May? 1956 – Kit Carson, Taos
June 22, 1956 – Nike, Carrizozo

June 4, 1957 – Zuni, Gallup

May 1, 1958 – Yucca, Spencerville
May 1958 – Sahara, Grants
May 29, 1958 – Pueblo, Santa Fe
Aug. 22, 1958 – Comet, Clovis

May 7, 1959 – Downs, Ruidoso Downs
1959? – Frontier, Regina

May? 1960 – Fort Union, Las Vegas
June 28, 1960 – Big Sky, Carlsbad
1960? – Kelly's / Rainbow / Chama, Chama

Jan. 26, 1962 – Wyoming, Albuquerque

June 19, 1963 – Circle Autoscope, Albuquerque
1963? – Cactus, Roswell
Nov. 6, 1963 – Silver Dollar, Albuquerque

May 12, 1966 – Aggie, Las Cruces

April 21, 1978 – Albuquerque 6, Albuquerque

1979? – Placita Hills, Cuba

Drive-Ins by City

Alamogordo

The closest city to the White Sands National Park, (recently upgraded from a national monument), Alamogordo saw its population grow from under 4000 in 1940 to over 20,000 in 1960. Holloman Air Force Base, established a few miles outside of town in 1942, was a large reason for the influx of residents, which provided enough viewers to support two local drive-ins.

Starlite Drive-In

Location: Two miles west of town on US 70
Opened: Dec. 9, 1949
Closed: Sept. 24, 1983
Capacity: 400 cars

Marshall Sanguinet came to Alamogordo from Fort Worth TX in June 1949 thanks to his company's building contracts for nearby Holloman Air Force Base. Apparently he fell in love with the place, and in September, he announced that he would build a drive-in theater and a new house adjacent to it for his family.

When the Starlite opened, it had a 50x40-foot screen 20 feet off the ground

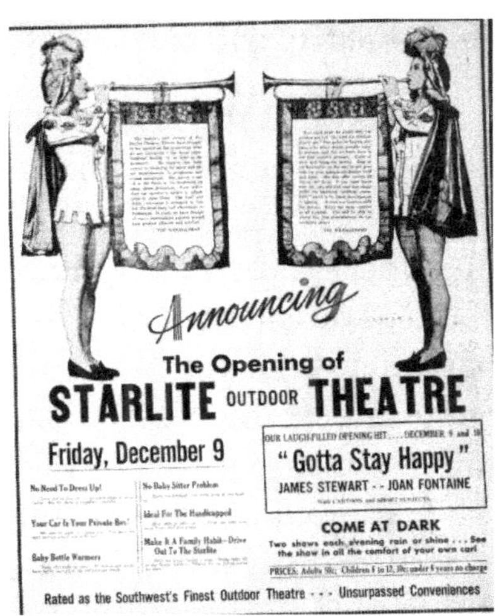

The Starlite bought a full-page ad in the *Alamogordo News* for its grand opening.

and was paved with asphalt. Artificial moonlight lit the viewing field, and its refreshment stand was "arranged to serve cars as they arrive, or during the show," according to the *Alamogordo News*. I'm not sure what that looked like.

In early 1952, Sanguinet sold the Starlite to Theatre Enterprises, owners of the indoor Mesa and White Sands theaters. That company would become Frontier Theatres, which was bought by Commonwealth Theatres, the Starlite's final owner. The site was never redeveloped after it closed; the ramps are still visible today.

Sanguinet announced in December 1952 that he was running for Alamogordo city commissioner, but it turned out that he filed his paperwork too late for the election. He left town soon after that to work on overseas construction projects, dying in Pakistan in 1967.

Yucca Drive-In

Location: Two miles north of town on US 70/54
Opened: Feb. 2, 1954
Closed: Oct. 27, 1974
Capacity: 450 cars

Business must have been good at the Starlite Drive-In, because owner Marshall Sanguinet decided to build another on the north side of town. At a city council meeting in April 1952, he requested a city water connection 330 feet outside the city limits. After the commissioners balked at sending water out of town at the local rate, Sanguinet immediately asked for his land to be annexed into the city.

After construction started, something about the water hookup was challenging enough to stop work. During that down period, Sanguinet sold the project along with the Starlite to Theatre Enterprises. Work resumed on the Yucca a year and a half later, and the drive-in had a 62x44-

foot screen when it opened. Manager Clifford Keim was proud of the Yucca's plug-in speakers, which were handed out at the box office and collected when cars exited. Keim said the speakers would produce better sound if kept in storage when not in use; he didn't mention how the system also reduced speaker vandalism and theft.

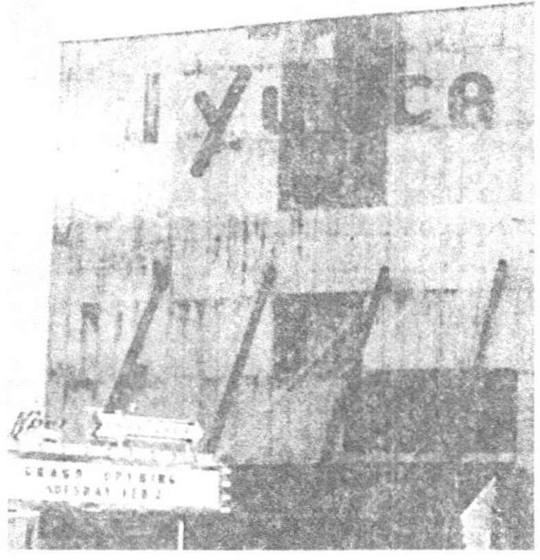

The *Alamogordo News* ran this photo of the Yucca's screen tower the week before the drive-in opened.

From there, the Yucca lived a quiet, corporate life. Its final movie ad in the *Alamogordo Daily News* appeared in October 1974. It ran a classified ad in March 1975 for concession stand help, and it joined other local businesses in congratulating the graduating high school class in May, but it apparently didn't reopen. Workers toppled the Yucca's sturdy screen tower in 1981 to make way for construction of a Sierra Ice & Water warehouse, though Commonwealth continued to include the Yucca in its list of theaters through 1984.

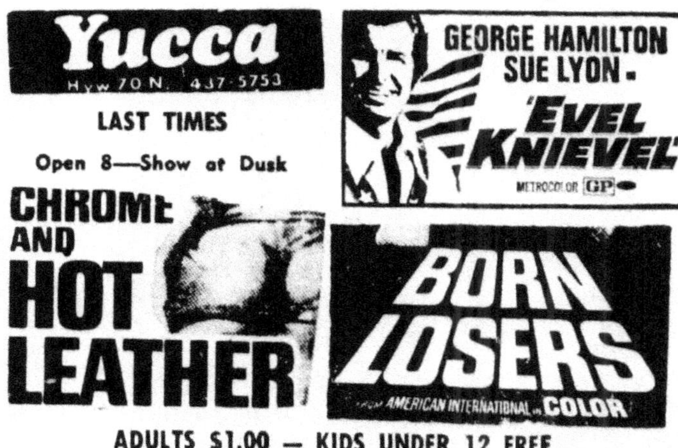

A 1972 Yucca ad from the *Alamogordo Daily News*.

Albuquerque

Over a quarter of the people who live in New Mexico today live in Albuquerque. Its temperate climate and booming population resulted in a lot of drive-ins. For a couple of weeks in November 1963, there were 11 active ozoners in Albuquerque.

66 Drive-In

Location: Next to the old West Mesa Airport just west of town on US 66 (Central Avenue)
Opened: Aug. 30, 1949
Closed: June 25, 1983
Capacity: 750 cars

Albuquerque Theatres must have liked the response to the city's first two drive-ins, because they soon jumped on the bandwagon. Its local manager, George Tucker, said in February 1949 that the 66 Drive-In, at the entrance to the old West Mesa Airport, would hold about 750 to 1000 cars. In April, he added that the drive-in would open with in-car heaters, and in May, he dropped the planned capacity

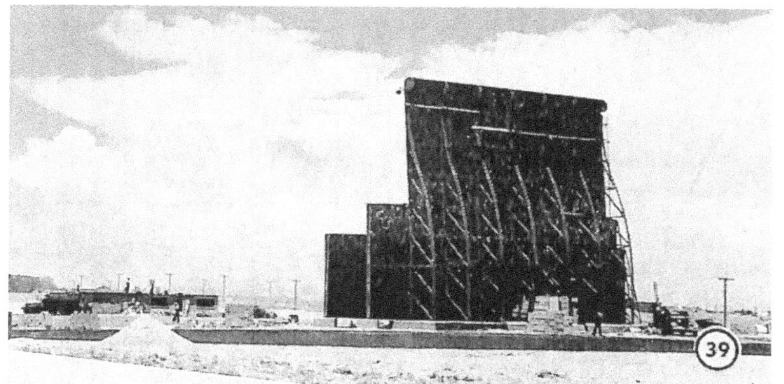

The Albuquerque National Bank, in its monthly *Albuquerque Progress,* published this photo of the 66 in 1949 while it was still under construction.

to 550 cars. That was its size when the 66 opened, complete with a patio next to the snack bar for patrons who wanted to watch the movie outside their cars.

In the early days, before more competing drive-ins opened, the 66 often played to capacity crowds. Its ad in the June 11, 1951 *Albuquerque Journal* boasted that the drive-in had added room for another 200 cars as a result. That would probably mark the high point in the 66's history.

In the spring of 1957, just six years after the 66 expanded its viewing field, Albuquerque Theatres replaced it with the "66 Micro-Midget Race Track," a tenth-mile car-racing oval and grandstands costing $150,000. That fad didn't last long. In the summer of 1962, the company announced that, with more folks moving to the west side of town, it would effectively rebuild the 66 as a drive-in again. By the time it reopened in July 1964, Frontier Theatres had bought the place. Frontier installed a new sign and a new 50x100-foot screen.

In 1968, Common-wealth Theatres bought out Frontier, including the 66. Around 1980, Common-wealth subleased the drive-in to Texas National Theaters,

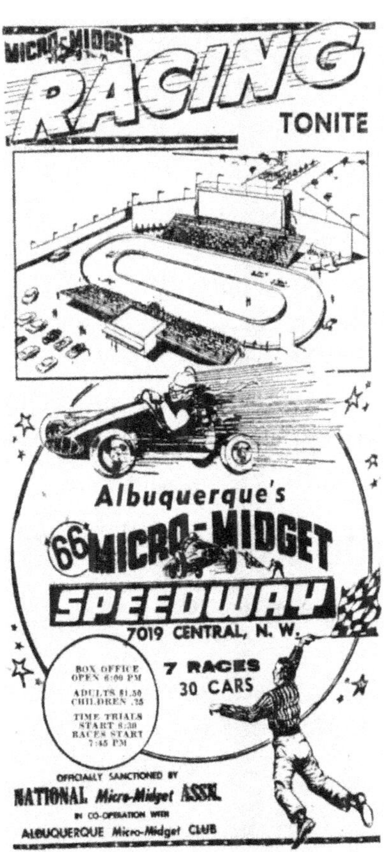

This ad from the *Albuquerque Journal* suggests what those Micro-Midget races were like.

which emphasized "skin flicks" in its nightly shows.
Prompted by unhappy neighbors, the city of Albuquerque
said the drive-in was operating in violation of the zoning
code, which prohibited adult entertainment within 500 feet
of residences, churches, or schools. In September 1980, the
city obtained a permanent injunction against showing such
films, and the state supreme court upheld that injunction
in January 1982.

Texas National soon struck back, requesting the city's
permission to divide its land, which would put the theater
section far enough away from nearby residences. When
that failed, the company filed a federal lawsuit asserting its
First Amendment right to choose what movies to show.
The city settled with Texas National that summer, agreeing
to assume the remaining two years of the company's lease
at a cost of $145,000. Racing returned to the site for those
two summers; the park department used it as a BMX dirt
bike track.

The 66 sat idle for years after the city's lease expired.
In the late 1990s, a food distribution company built a
warehouse in the back of the field; two expansions later,
it's still there today.

Albuquerque 6 Drive-In

Location: North of I-25 just west of the Jefferson Street
exit
Opened: April 21, 1978
Closed: Sept. 17, 1995
Capacity: 3800 cars

Raymond Syufy, the son of Lebanese immigrants,
opened his first movie theater in Vallejo CA in 1941. He
expanded Syufy Theaters into a regional chain, eventually
operating over 170 screens, mostly in California and

Nevada. In 1978, Syufy looked to expand eastward. The company picked a spot just off I-25 on the north side of Albuquerque and started construction in February 1978.

When the Albuquerque 6 opened two months later, it was the largest drive-in complex the city would ever see. Its lots were equipped with in-car heaters, reportedly on every speaker pole. The central, two-story projection hub featured a cafeteria-style concession stand on its ground floor and a children's playground outside.

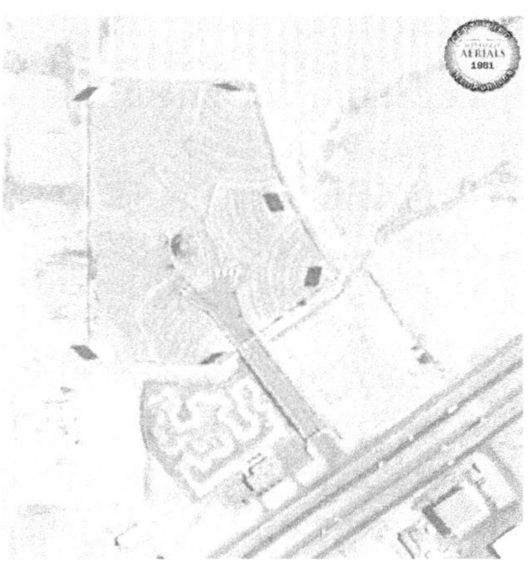

This 1981 aerial view of the Albuquerque 6 shows the central projection building and the six different-sized viewing fields. © HistoricAerials.com, used by permission.

The 6 lived a quiet, corporate-owned life. Syufy Theaters opened its first "Century 21" quasi-futuristic indoor theater in 1964, and changed its name to Century Theatres by the early 1990s.

In October 1995, a month after the 6's final shows, Century got the city's approval to bulldoze the drive-in and built what became the indoor Century Rio 24-plex, which is still there today.

If you really want to know what the Albuquerque 6 looked like, head west to the suburbs of Phoenix, where Syufy built the Glendale 9 Drive-In a year after the Albuquerque 6 opened. Glendale's version boasts the same central, two-story projection and concession building and a similar scattering of screens, and it's still in operation as Arizona's last active drive-in.

Cactus Drive-In

Location: On Yale Boulevard less than a half mile north of Gibson Boulevard
Opened: Sept. 26, 1947
Closed: Sept. 28, 1975
Capacity: 680 cars

The first large drive-in in New Mexico was built by George Tucker and Albuquerque Theaters in late 1947. Its sturdy screen tower was made of welded steel pipes, with a manager's office, storage space, and a three-room caretaker's apartment at the base. On the screen side, a children's playground and outdoor seating faced a 45x55-foot screen. Its concession stand, 250 feet away in the center of the fourth ramp, was decorated in green and coral.

When the Cactus opened, patrons would buy tickets at the box office, then drive around a cactus garden to ushers who would direct them to their parking spaces, equipped with RCA in-car speakers. In 1949, the Cactus added in-car heaters.

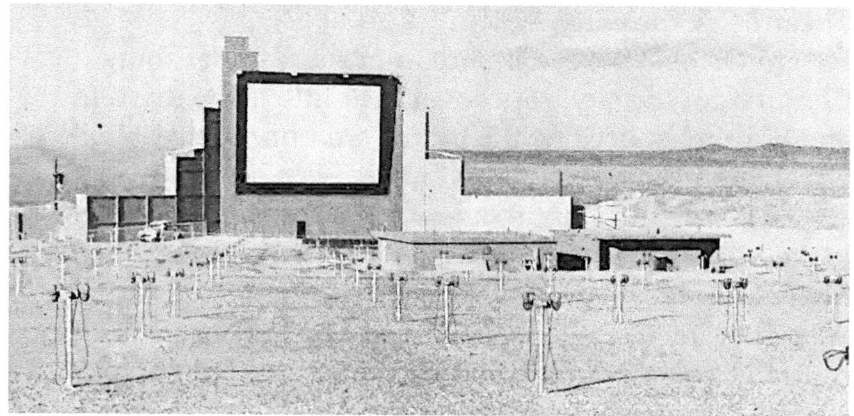

In 1948, *Motion Picture Herald* ran several photos of the newly opened Cactus Drive-In. This one shows the projection-concession buildings facing the black-edged screen.

The drive-in's ownership changes confuse me – feel free to skip this paragraph. By 1956, Henry Griffith was president of Albuquerque Exhibitors, which owned the Cactus among other theaters. In January that year, Dallas-based Frontier Theaters, of which Griffith was also president, bought Albuquerque Exhibitors. In 1959, Video Independent Theatres of Oklahoma began operating the Cactus. Then in the summer of 1962, Albuquerque Theatres, still a subsidiary of Frontier, took over the Cactus from All-States Theatres. Commonwealth Theatres bought out Frontier in 1968, and that's who owned the Cactus when it closed.

The drive-in's gorgeous screen tower stayed up for several years after the Cactus closed. In 1983, the city bought the site to replace the Heights Community Center. Today the Loma Linda Community Center lives there, with faint hints of the drive-in's back ramps on the east side.

Circle Autoscope Drive-In

Location: One block north of the Duke City Drive-In on Carlisle Boulevard near Candelaria Road
Opened: June 19, 1963
Closed: Dec. 1, 1963
Capacity: 254 cars

The Circle Autoscope prompts a metaphysical question: What is a drive-in theater? Is it a place where lots of cars come to watch the same movie? If so, then the Circle fits. Do the cars all need to point at a large, common screen? If that's the case, then the Circle didn't qualify. The Circle, like other Autoscopes, projected its movies on dozens of smaller screens, one per car.

Tom Smith invented the Autoscope, opening the first 42-screen version in his home town of Urbana MO in 1953.

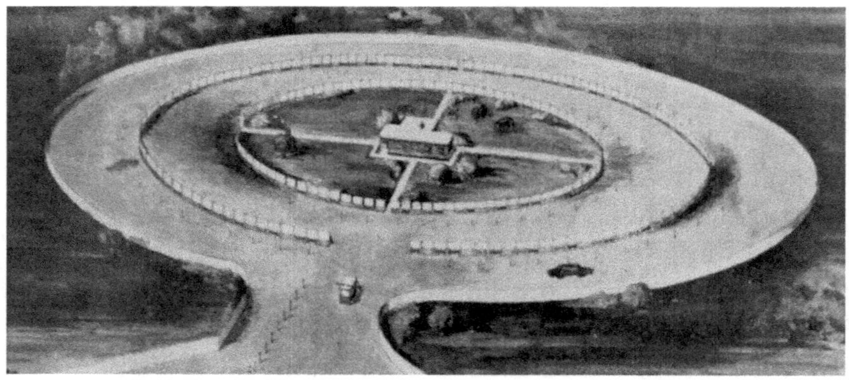

This artist's rendering of the then-future Autoscope project is the best illustration I've found for the concentric Circle Drive-In. It was published in *Boxoffice* magazine.

The idea was simple – instead of building one huge screen, build a circle of much smaller screens. The execution of that idea was extremely complicated, requiring an elaborate system of mirrors and lenses, but Smith worked it all out. In 1954, Smith built a 125-screen Autoscope in Buffalo MO. The sudden popularity of widescreen movies apparently sent Smith back to his inventor's bench. In 1960, he widened Buffalo's screens.

Albuquerque's Circle was, as far as I can tell, the largest Autoscope ever built. Its 3x5-foot screens were arranged in two concentric circles, one five feet higher and 50 feet farther from the center building, which included a snack bar and playground.

Despite its unique offering, the Circle closed the same year that it opened. Ironically, *Life* magazine came by in September 1963 to shoot photos, but it didn't publish them until after the Circle's final performance. My guess is that the Autoscope was doomed by the city's glut of active drive-ins at the time; newspaper ads in the fall of 1963 reflected a serious ticket price war. Building the Circle so close to the decade-old Duke City probably didn't help.

Not only is there no trace of the Circle today, aerial

photos suggest it was replaced with apartments almost immediately after closing. For more about Autoscopes in general, check out the intermission between Aztec and Belen.

Duke City Drive-In

Location: On Carlisle Boulevard one block north of Menaul Boulevard
 Opened: Feb. 17, 1953
 Closed: Sept. 3, 1979
 Capacity: 600 cars

In October 1952, on the first anniversary of the opening of the Terrace, owner Tom Griffing announced that he would build another Albuquerque drive-in. Construction proceeded faster than anticipated, and only cool weather delayed the opening until mid-February.

The Duke City Drive-In, a moniker taken from the nickname of its host city, included red-lighted stop signs along a center pedestrian path to the concession stand, which featured modern self-service. The projection booth was future-proofed with facilities for 3D and TV-based projectors, although those fads died out within a few years.

In the summer of 1953, manager George Fossell

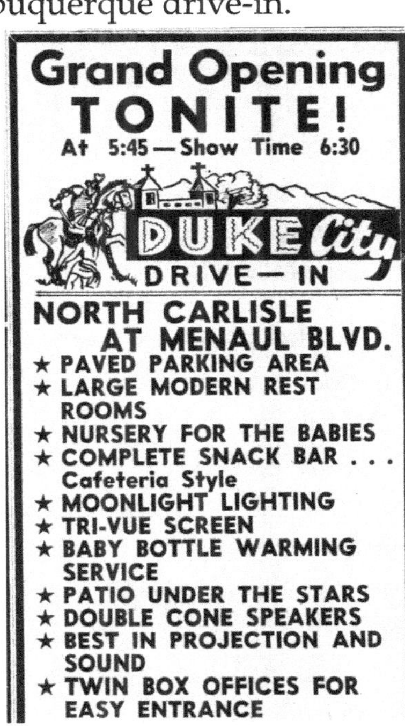

The top of the Duke City's grand opening ad, as it appeared in the *Albuquerque Journal*.

showed off special nozzles, which were on every speaker post, for the *Albuquerque Journal*. Workers used the sprayers to distribute a disinfectant-insecticide mixture every day that summer, taking four hours a day to get through all 600 spots in the viewing lot.

The Duke City lived a relatively quiet life, owned by Griffing's All-States Theatres. Oklahoma-based Video Independent Theatres bought All-States' drive-ins in early 1963. VIT installed a self-service car wash out front in 1964, planted hundreds of trees in a 1966 landscaping project, added an exit guard in 1968, and repaired the flexiboard on the screen tower after a 1969 storm. The Duke City quietly closed on Labor Day 1979, then didn't reopen in 1980. A Walmart occupies the site today.

San Jose / Tri-C / Route 25 Drive-In

Location: On Broadway Boulevard about a half mile south of Woodward Road
   Opened: Feb. 23, 1954
   Closed: June 18, 1965
   Capacity: 400 cars

Robert Morley owned a small piece of Albuquerque's Sunset Drive-In. It must have been doing well because in September 1953, he began building his own drive-in on the east side of the Rio Grande. Morley claimed that the San Jose's screen, 85x70 feet, was one of the largest in the Southwest, and that its lot would hold 600 cars. By the time the drive-in opened, its size was scaled back to 400 cars.

The San Jose started with a policy of double features including one Spanish-language movie and one in English. By the summer of 1955, it occasionally showed what the Catholic Legion of Decency called "very dirty" movies; Morley defended them as "highly educational" hygiene

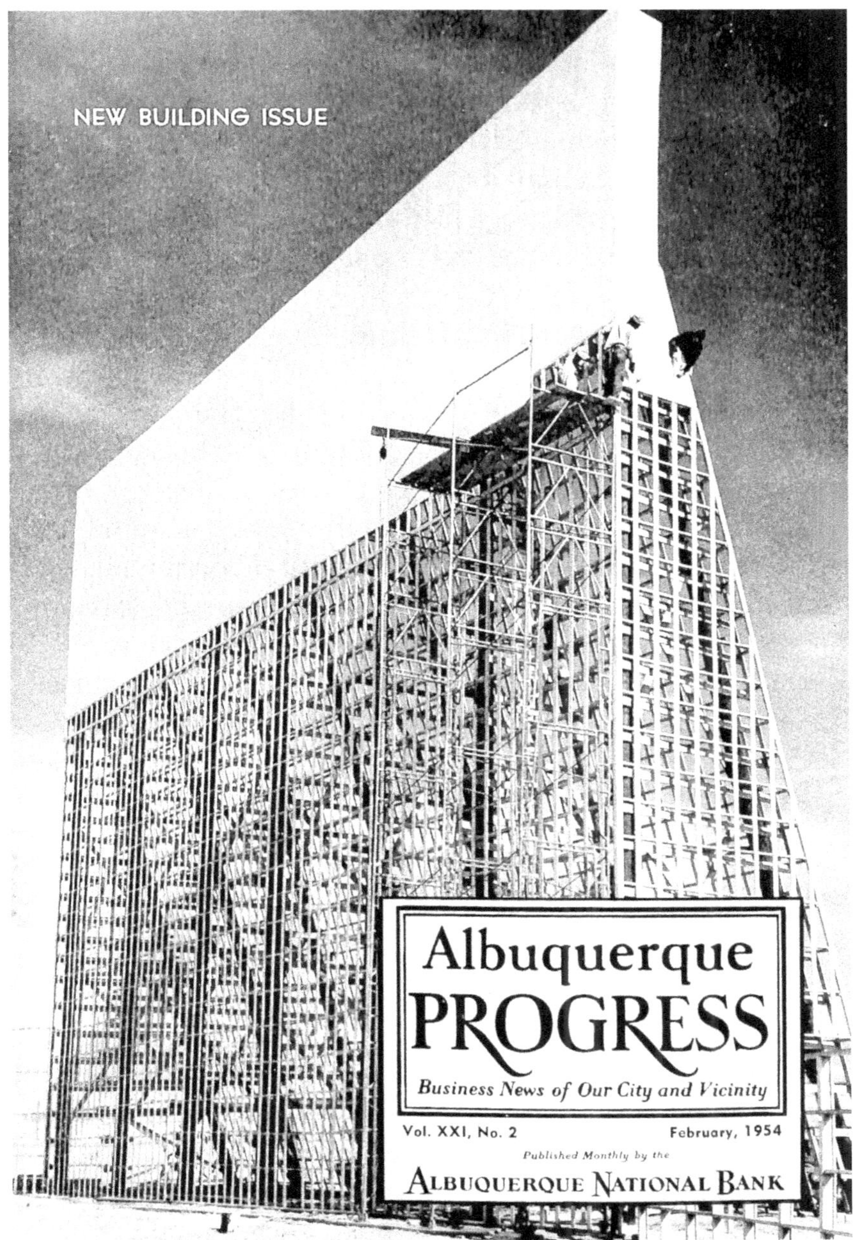

The enormity of the San Jose Drive-In's screen tower building
project was captured on the cover of the *Albuquerque Progress*,
published by Albuquerque National Bank. Although it looked
sturdy, that tower was flattened by winds just nine years later.

films. In September 1956, the San Jose was hit with an injunction against showing allegedly indecent films.

The following spring, Morley sold the San Jose to Carl Halberg, who renamed it the Tri-C. Just a few weeks later, winds blew down chunks of the screen, which Halberg quickly patched. In October 1957, the New Mexico Supreme Court overruled the year-old injunction because the relevant statute didn't apply to movies.

In the summer of 1961, Halberg leased the Tri-C to Sero Amusement of Los Angeles, which ran it for about two years. In the spring of 1963, winds knocked down the old screen, and Halberg replaced it with a metal screen, reopening in June as the Route 25 Drive-In. The site's high winds had the last laugh just two years later, pushing the metal screen backward at a 45-degree angle on the night of June 18, 1965. Apparently, that was when Halberg gave up. The Route 25 never ran another ad in the *Albuquerque Journal* after that night, and a 1967 aerial photo showed the site overgrown. A truck salvage yard is there today.

Silver Dollar Drive-In

Location: On San Mateo Boulevard less than a mile south of I-25
Opened: Nov. 6, 1963
Closed: Sept. 2, 1980
Capacity: 800 cars

Tom Griffing's All States Theaters was looking to expand into suburban areas when it bought a 50-acre site in late 1961. Construction of the Silver Dollar didn't start until the fall of 1963. General manager Paul West said at the time that the drive-in would open with a single screen but would have a second screen the following year. By the time it opened, Video Theaters had acquired the Silver Dollar, though West remained in charge.

Despite the earlier plan, the Silver Dollar operated for over a decade with just one screen on the north side of its lot. In July 1975, West oversaw construction of two smaller screens in the southwest and southeast corners, then reopened the Silver Dollar as the state's first three-screen drive-in in September 1975.

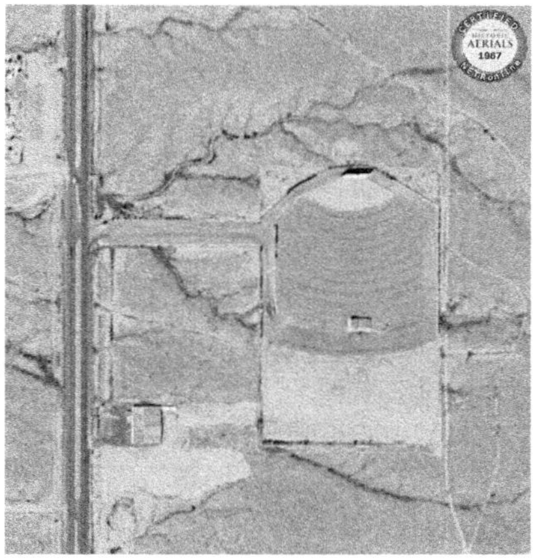

In its early years, such as this 1967 photo, the Silver Dollar was by itself. Now the site is surrounded by housing and offices. © HistoricAerials.com, used by permission.

That's pretty much the end of the story. The Silver Dollar led a quiet, corporate-owned life, staying away from the adult entertainment that filled some of the city's other outdoor screens. It quietly closed on the day after Labor Day, 1980, and never reopened. An apartment complex, the Villas at La Privada, occupies the site today.

Star / Linda Vista /Northside Drive-In

Location: On 2nd Street just south of Montano Road
Opened: July 27, 1949
Closed: Nov. 12, 1988
Capacity: 500 cars

Now here was a drive-in with several distinct lives. The first started with former and future concrete aggregate manufacturer Thomas E. Ribble, who took a break from that career to build and operate the Star Drive-In. The only note I found of the Star's early years came when a show was interrupted by a nearby sawdust fire, which was quickly extinguished by city firefighters. Ribble was popular enough to be elected president of the New Mexico

Theatre Association in 1952, but perhaps he tired of the business. Before the 1956 season, Ribble sold the Star to local theater man Marlin Butler, who also owned the Sunset and Tesuque drive-ins.

Sometime during the 1960-61 offseason, a windstorm blew down the Star's screen. The drive-in remained closed for over a year until Albuquerque Theatres stepped in and rebuilt it, reopening on Sept. 19, 1962. By 1968, the Star was showing Spanish-language films. It closed in

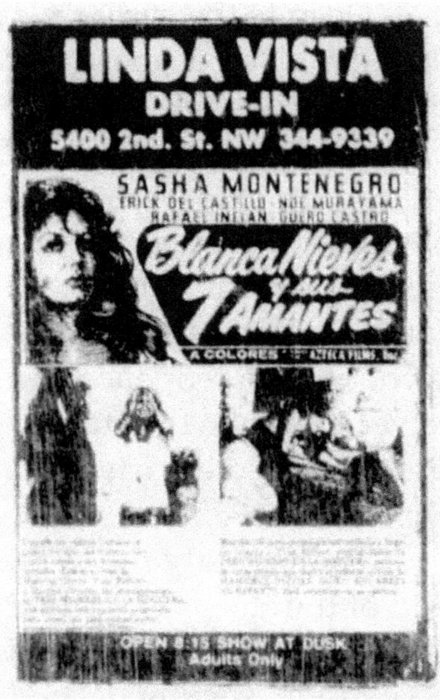

A typical Linda Vista Drive-In ad, from a 1983 edition of the *Albuquerque Journal*.

December that year, and new owners Commonwealth Theatres soon announced that it would not reopen in 1969 "since the lease runs out on May 1."

The drive-in's second life came a few months later after Mel Sanchez took over, reopening it as the Linda Vista in the summer of 1969. It continued to show films in Spanish with occasional ads in the local English-language newspapers until at least 1983.

The third and final life was shepherded by Curtis and Melinda Ralston, a married couple who had met years earlier while working at the Silver Dollar Drive-In. They leased Sanchez's drive-in in September 1986, reopening it as the Northside. The Ralstons showed mostly English-language features for over two years, until the drive-in closed for good after the 1988 season. The former Star site is now home to a police station.

Sunset Drive-In

Location: On Arenal Road just west of Goff/Isleta Boulevard
   Opened: Nov. 28, 1951
   Closed: Sept. 1, 1990
   Capacity: 400 cars

Longtime theater owner Marlin Butler announced at the end of August 1951 that the National Production Authority had granted him permission to build a small drive-in to serve the Armijo neighborhood. The Sunset was constructed in three months, opening on the Wednesday after Thanksgiving.

The Sunset lived a quiet life for a few years until Butler sold or leased it to Carl and Phyllis Halberg, who also purchased the San Jose / Tri-C across the river in 1957. In 1963, Sero Amusement of California, the company booking the Tri-C's movies, ran into local opposition for their racy content. Around the same time, residents near the Sunset, which happened to be just outside the city limits, lodged a similar complaint about its films. Phyllis told the *Albuquerque Journal* that "an out of town

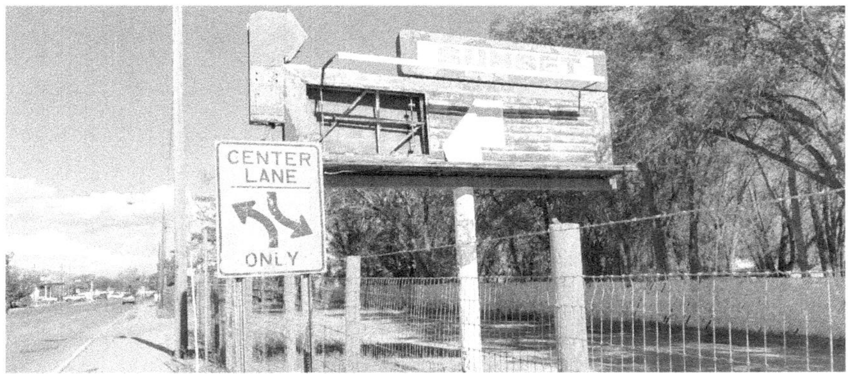

The old Sunset Drive-In sign was hanging in there, just barely, in this 2019 photo by the author.

company" was booking the Sunset's movies, and a few weeks later, Carl issued a statement that he had ended the "lease arrangement with an unnamed man in California."

By the end of 1963, Butler's business partner Fred Morley filed a lawsuit against the Halbergs seeking to reclaim the Sunset. The suit probably went well, because in August 1968, Butler sold the drive-in to Commonwealth-Frontier Theatres. Under Commonwealth, the drive-in showed mostly Spanish-language movies until it closed after the 1981 season.

Someone reopened the Sunset in 1987, showing mostly English-language films. The 1988 *Motion Picture Almanac* listed the owner as "D. Armino," probably a misspelling of David Armijo, who had always owned the Sunset's land. That version of the drive-in continued until at least the 1990 season. The screen and the remains of the marquee are still there today, although its concession stand and ramps were leveled in late 2020.

Terrace Drive-In

Location: On US 66 (Central Avenue) on the east side of town
Opened: Oct. 18, 1951
Closed: Jan. 20, 1980
Capacity: 1600 cars

Tom Griffing was a prolific drive-in builder for other owners, and occasionally he would keep one for himself. So it was with the Terrace, named for the terrace of 400 lounge chairs that Griffing provided for patrons who wanted to leave their cars. Despite Korean War-time restrictions on the use of certain materials, Griffing kept the project under the copper maximum (barely) by running heavy wiring directly from the utility poles to the top of the projection booth, which was on top of the concession stand at the back of the viewing field. There wasn't enough copper left to reach the exit lights, so the Terrace got by with kerosene lanterns until they were free to run more wiring.

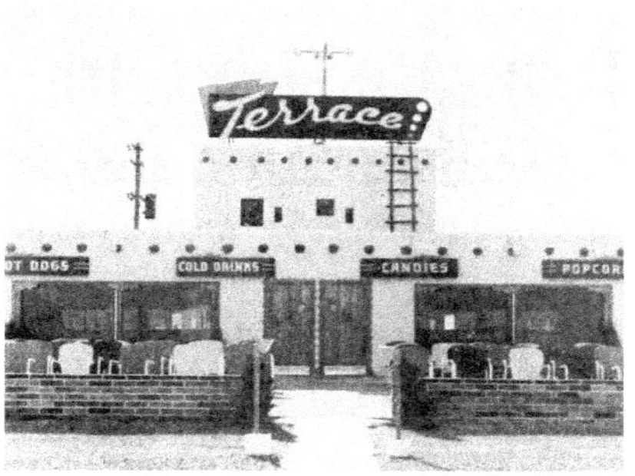

Motion Picture Herald published this photo of the newly opened Terrace Drive-In.

Just a year later, Griffing added a second screen, advertising the drive-in as the Terrace Twin. For the first few decades, the Terrace would show the same double feature on both screens, playing one movie first on one screen, the other movie first on the second screen. The expansion doubled the drive-in's capacity to 1600 cars, large enough to stage several "drive-in world premieres" over the years.

In early 1963, Griffing's All-States Theatres sold its 11 drive-ins in New Mexico and Texas to Video Independent Theatres of Oklahoma. The new owners rewired the car speakers in 1968 and fixed tornado damage on its neon sign in 1969. Finally, in 1975, VIT recognized that it could run completely separate double features on its two screens. The Terrace closed for the season in January 1980 and didn't reopen. A mobile home park occupies the site today.

I saved the best part of the Terrace for last. Artist Keith Kent designed and neon worker Doug Mason constructed a 70-foot-high dancing woman on the back of the screen tower. An *Albuquerque Journal* columnist later remembered it as "a queen of the tubes, an empress of electricity, who presided over this phosphorescent firmament." I'd love to see more color photos and movies of that neon in its prime.

Tesuque Drive-In

Location: At the corner of Pennsylvania Avenue and what was then Tesuque Street, where Mesa Verde Park is today
Opened: Aug. 7, 1949
Closed: Dec. 13, 1977
Capacity: 656 cars

The Tesuque, Albuquerque's second drive-in, went through more changes than any other drive-in in New Mexico. When it opened, it had a single screen facing north and a narrow lot that held just 368 cars. Business was so good that in 1952, owners Clifford and Helen Butler made a deal with Helen's brother, Earle E. Unger, to finance an expansion that included a second screen. The couple would later say they agreed to let Unger represent himself as sole owner of the Tesuque to facilitate loans; I'm sure Unger told a different story.

In 1953, the Tesuque expanded to two screens serving 850 cars. That was also the year Unger incorporated the Tesuque Drive-In Theatres, with himself as president, his wife as vice-president, manager W. T. Marshall as secretary-treasurer, and the Butlers out of the picture. The couple sued. In July 1954, a court ruled that the Butlers' real estate contracts with Unger were legitimate, so the Tesuque corporation won. The Butlers divorced in January 1956.

I'm not sure whether it was related to the aftermath of the lawsuit, but 1954 was also when the Tesuque was sold to Sunset Drive-In owner Marlin Butler, apparently no relation to Clifford. In February 1956, a windstorm tore off a section of the Tesuque's east screen. Butler rebuilt the east screen later that year, but scrapped it for the 1957 season.

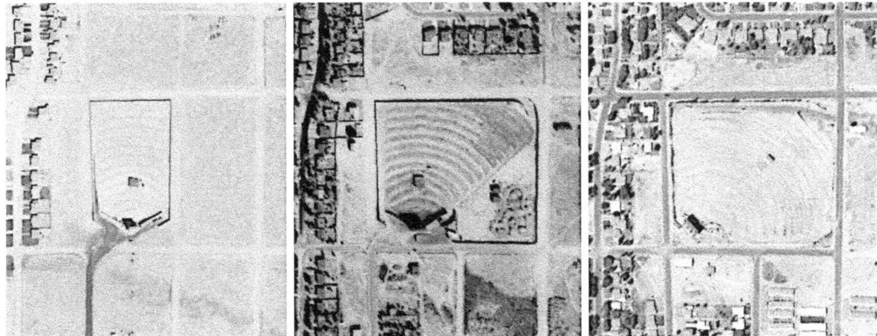

The changing outlines of the Tesuque are evident in these three aerial photos. On the left (1951), how the drive-in started. The center photo (1959) came after a second screen was built in the northeast corner and later removed. The right photo (1967) shows the Tesuque's final configuration after moving its screen tower. © HistoricAerials.com, used by permission.

The removal of the second screen left a single viewing area with a lot of its cars awkwardly positioned at an angle to the remaining screen. The Tesuque fixed this with the unusual step of rotating the original screen about 45 degrees to face northeast. In 1958, Butler also enlarged the concession stand to reflect the larger field. At the end of 1963, he sold the Tesuque to Frontier Theatres on a lease-purchase agreement. Commonwealth Theatres bought out Frontier in 1968. By 1971, it was running the Tesuque as a cut-rate dollar theater.

The Tesuque had been built in a vacant area outside of town, but through the decades, housing had expanded to surround the site. By the mid-1970s, the neighborhood association lobbied the city to buy and close the drive-in, calling it a blight "because of ugly signs and because it attracts persons from outside the neighborhood." The association got its wish in 1978; the local Urban Development Agency used federal funds to acquire the Tesuque, which it converted to the Mesa Verde Park and Community Center, still there today.

Wyoming Drive-In

Location: On US 66 (Central Avenue), adjacent to the
Terrace
   Opened: Jan. 26, 1962
   Closed: Sept. 18, 1978
   Capacity: 1000 cars

As Albuquerque grew in the 1950s, the Terrace Drive-
In eventually became an unincorporated enclave,
surrounded by the city. That's probably why the Wyoming
was built as a separate drive-in rather than the Terrace's
third screen – it was always within the city limits. Tom
Griffing came out of semi-retirement to build the
Wyoming, which had a 120x60-foot screen and a four-lane
cafeteria-style concession stand. *Boxoffice* reported in
November 1961 that the drive-in had opened on
Thanksgiving Day, but that announcement was premature.

Griffing's company, All-States Theatres, owned the
Wyoming for barely a year
before selling it with their
other 10 drive-ins to Oklahoma-based Video Indepen-
dent Theatres. Just before
Christmas 1967, strong
winds smashed over 500 feet
of the Wyoming's fence and
broke some glass in its sign.
Video resurfaced the lot
along with the Terrace's in
1968. In early 1969, part of
the fence was blown down
again.

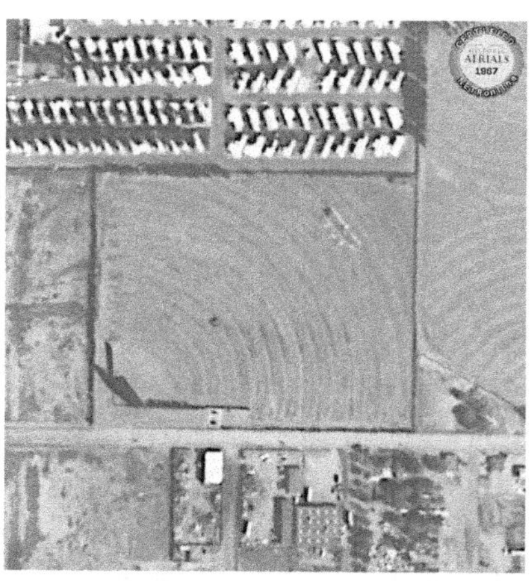

The eastern fence between the
Wyoming (center) and the
Terrace Twin Drive-In (right)
was also an Albuquerque city
border. © HistoricAerials.com,
used by permission.

The Wyoming closed at
the end of the 1978 season, a

victim of rising land values. A mobile home park occupies the site today.

Anthony

This small town, just across the border from the El Paso TX metropolitan area, didn't incorporate until 2010. Spanish speakers make up the great majority of its residents, which is a big reason why its drive-in, the southernmost in New Mexico, favored Spanish-language films.

Joy Drive-In

Location: On Highway 478 about two miles northwest of town
Opened: April? 1954
Closed: 1977?
Capacity: 300 cars

For the Joy, I have a lot more questions than answers.

When did it open? Raymond Parsons, who bought Anthony's indoor New-Tex Theater in September 1953, reportedly planned to build a drive-in "on the outskirts" of town. Did that become the Joy? Its first ad in the *El Paso Times* was on May 5, 1954, but looked nothing like a Grand Opening; it promoted its $1 carload pricing.

The 1955-56 *Theatre Catalog* listed the Joy's owner as H. R. Poor, who owned theaters in Lawn TX almost 500 miles away. Tom Griffing bought the Joy near the end of 1956. The 1960 *Motion Picture Almanac* said the owners were "Hanson & Moore." And that's most of what I know. In 1964, one

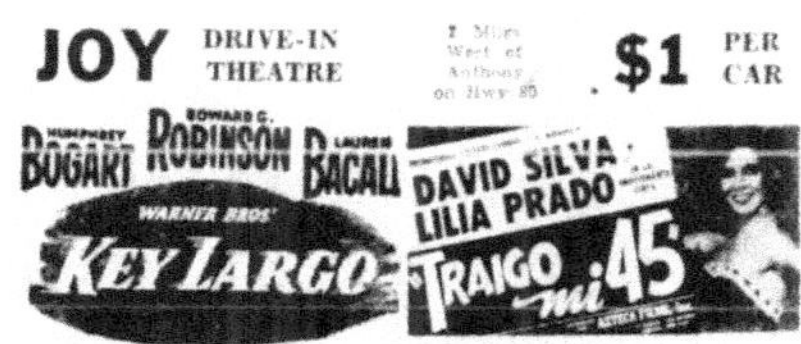

Possibly the Joy's first ad in the *El Paso Times*, from 1954.

18-year-old at the Joy reportedly killed another 18-year-old by stabbing him 17 times.

When did the Joy close? The last newspaper ad I could find was in 1974 and featured Spanish-language films, which may explain its infrequent appearances in English-language newspapers. A 1977 photo, now at the New Mexico History Museum, showed the apparently active Joy with its sign and Spanish-language movie posters in good repair.

At least part of the Joy stayed intact until around 1980. A *Times* article published in 1988 said that "eight years ago" sisters Bertha Rizzuti and Ernestina Acosta converted the former Joy's snack bar "on their family's farm" to a preschool classroom. As of this writing, that's all I know.

Arenas Valley

Arenas Valley is a census-designated place with its own ZIP code. Its status was tenuous enough that all references to Arenas Valley's drive-in, from before it opened through the final notes in the 1970s, said that it was by Silver City.

Copper / Sundowner Drive-In

Location: On US 180, about six miles east of Silver City, about 2.5 miles west of Santa Clara
Opened: August? 1951
Closed: 1982?
Capacity: 400 cars

Ray and Herbert Johnson opened their 400-car, $60,000 drive-in in the summer of 1951. One *Boxoffice* report said that the Copper Drive-In had opened in July; a later *Boxoffice* report said it had opened a short time before Labor Day. Located on the Silver City-Central highway east of Silver City, it was Grant County's first drive-in.

George Dowdle bought the Copper in early 1953. At some point, it was acquired by Dollison Theatres. That's who owned the Copper in June 1957 when a windstorm toppled the screen and a wall there. Dollison rebuilt and reopened in August that year.

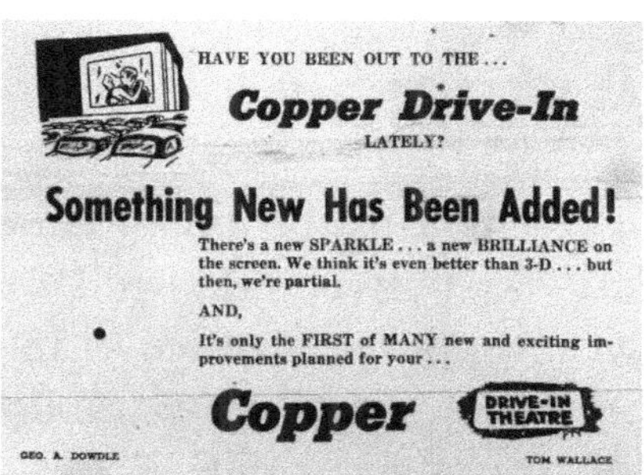

The Copper refreshed its screen in 1953, and promoted that fact in this ad in the *Silver City Daily Press*. I like it because it includes the owner and manager.

Les Dollison, owner of the chain, loved to rename his theaters now and then. It was the Copper's turn in 1966, when the drive-in reopened for the season as the Sundowner.

Moss Theatres, owned by James Moss, took over the Sundowner in late 1975. In 1978, the drive-in was the target of a new county pornography ordinance. Moss told county commissioners that he had planned to use a fence to block the view of the screen from US 180, but winds and rain had demolished the fence. He sued the company that built the fence.

In late 1979, Dollison reacquired the Sundowner from Moss. The drive-in continued to advertise through at least 1980, and a note from March 1982 in the *Deming Headlight* said that new Dollison regional manager Robert Bowen would be responsible for the indoor Gila and the Sundowner. Today the site hosts an odd assortment of small buildings.

Artesia

This city started as Miller, a railroad siding about halfway between Roswell and the future Carlsbad. When it picked up a post office in 1899, it officially became Stegman, named after the first postmistress. When Artesia incorporated in 1905, it was named for the then-plentiful artesian wells there.

Circle B Drive-In

Location: About two miles west of town on US 82
Opened: April 9, 1950
Closed: 1957?
Capacity: 350 cars

Ray Bartlett, who owned Artesia's indoor theaters, and his son Bill, who lived in Carlsbad, planned their first drive-in in the summer of 1949. Each speaker was to include "a heating element," which may have been an in-car heater. Construction continued into early 1950, and the Circle B opened on Easter Sunday. The drive-in had a red-and-yellow color scheme, and cattle brands decorated the concession stand. At the time it opened, vendors with pushcarts would bring some refreshments directly to patrons in their cars.

That July, Gary Blair was working at the exit gate before the movies started, making sure no one snuck in without going past the box office. One night, a small tornado lifted him from the ground and suspended him

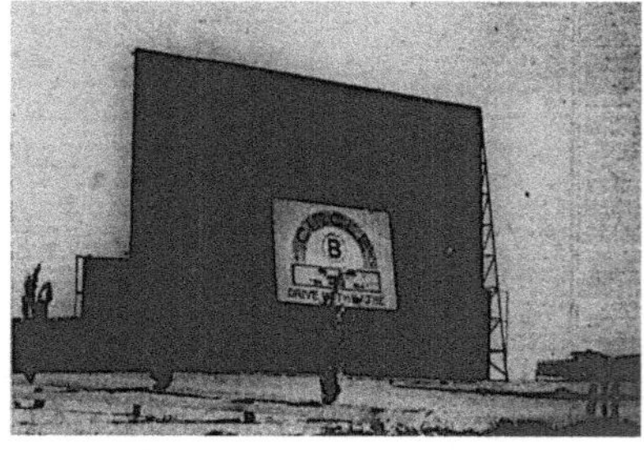

There's just enough legibility in this microfilm-stomped photo from the *Artesia Advocate* to suggest what the Circle B's screen tower looked like.

in the air as the concrete-anchored box office swayed. The wind left as quickly as it arrived, with no injuries or significant damage reported.

The Circle B remained in Artesia's telephone directories through just 1957, not long after the Hermosa opened, suggesting that Bartlett discovered that the city couldn't support two drive-ins. The Circle B was long gone in a 1983 aerial photo, replaced by a neighborhood of houses. Today, the only trace of the drive-in is a slab of its former entrance driveway on the shoulder of US 82 across from the fire station.

Hermosa Drive-In

Location: Just southeast of town on Hermosa Drive, one block west of US 285
Opened: Aug. 4, 1955
Closed: 1987?
Capacity: 350 cars

The Circle B must have done well for local theater man Ray Bartlett, because he bought the land for his second drive-in in late 1951. At the time, he said he would run movies first at one drive-in, then move them to the other. Because of a shortage of steel, Bartlett planned to build the screen tower out of wood, and he hoped to open on Easter again, this time in 1952.

I don't know why the project was delayed for over three years. The Artesia Historical Museum confirmed the Hermosa's 1955 opening date, which suggests that construction was delayed until that year. In

The *Artesia Advocate* included this photo of the Hermosa as part of a grand opening ad.

1960, Ray's son Bill Bartlett left his job managing theaters in Carlsbad after buying the Hermosa along with Artesia's indoor Landsun Theater. In 1972, former Artesia mayor Creighton Gilchrist purchased the Hermosa along with the Landsun.

And that's about all I know about the Hermosa. It continued to appear in the local telephone directory through 1987, and it was long gone in a 1997 aerial photo, replaced by the RV park that's still there today.

Aztec

Although dwarfed by nearby Farmington, Aztec is the seat of San Juan County, which includes them both. It used to be even smaller, but Aztec experienced an oil- and gas-related boom in the 1950s that led in part to the building of its only drive-in.

Rincon Drive-In

Location: Just east of town on Blanco Street
Opened: June 1, 1954
Closed: July 20, 1965?
Capacity: 250 cars

Zang Wood wrote in his booklet *Soda & Shows*, "After Porter and Bessie Smith moved from their ranch in Gobernador to their home on East Blanco Street in Aztec they built the Rincon Drive-In Theater on their property. It opened in the summer of 1953." I believe that date is a little off; the *Farmington Daily Times* ran an article on May 31, 1954 about the Rincon's grand opening the following night. The newspaper said the drive-in's seamless screen was built by the Canton Construction Company of Farmington, and that the owners were Mr. and Mrs. John Pettus, Mr. and Mrs. Ury Ealum, and the Smiths.

That's 90% of what I know about the Rincon. In April 1965, *Boxoffice* reported that Jim Paxton of Durango had taken over the drive-in. Its final ad in the *Daily Times* was on July 18 that year, advertising movies through the weekly Spanish-language night on the 20th. The Rincon's concession-projection building lingered into the 1990s, but the screen was down by 1971 and its hill was leveled in 1982 for installation of a house made of steel. There's no trace of it left today; the Creekside Village Court cul-de-sac occupies the former drive-in site.

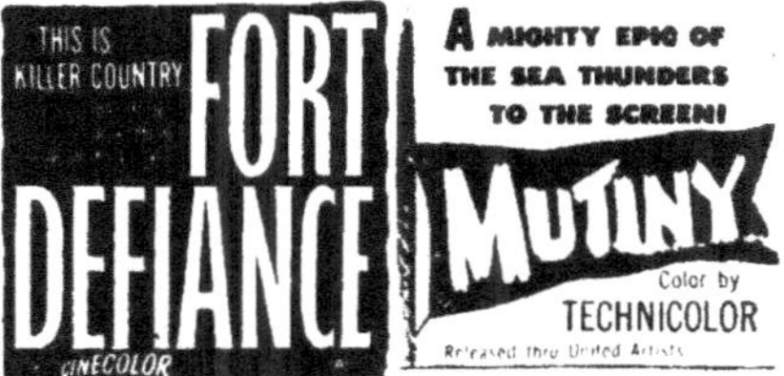

The Rincon's grand opening ad in the *Farmington Daily Times*.

Intermission: Autoscopes

New Mexico is known for all sorts of things, but no one ever points out that it was the home of the world's largest Autoscope. If you're asking, "What's an Autoscope?" then you didn't read the entry for Albuquerque's Circle Autoscope Drive-In a few pages ago.

As I wrote earlier, Tom Smith of Urbana MO invented the elaborate system of mirrors that delivered a single movie to a ring of screens, one per car. He claimed that his system gave every car a clearer, more equitable view of the movie, as opposed to viewers at the sides of a big-screen viewing field who saw a slanted version. Autoscopes required less land than conventional drive-ins, and they avoided the expensive construction and maintenance of a multistory screen tower. Each translucent screen was about

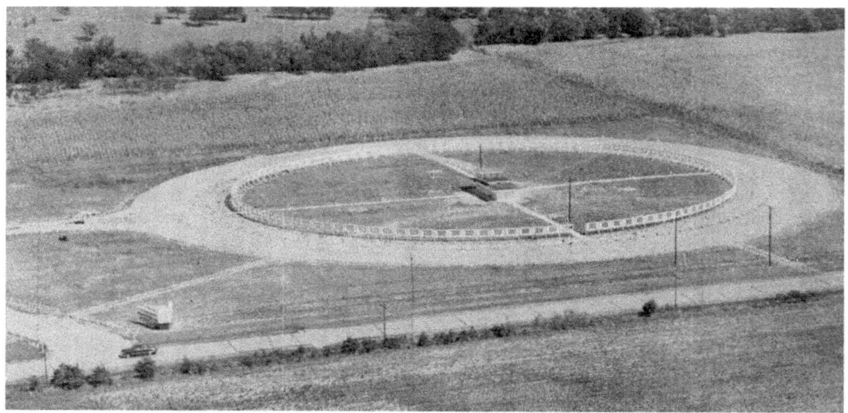

Tom Smith's second Autoscope, after his first experimental setup, was this drive-in in Buffalo MO. It included 125 screens.

the size of a flat-screen TV today, and they could be easily replaced if damaged.

Smith opened the first Autoscope in his hometown in 1953. It had a circle of 42 screens. The next year, he built what would become the standard size Autoscope, 125 screens, in Buffalo MO. Unfortunately for him, that was about when movie studios shifted to widescreen films, so he had to change all those mirrors. It took until 1960 for Buffalo's Autoscope to get upgraded to wide screens, and the next big experiment was in Albuquerque.

The Circle Autoscope was, in my opinion, Smith's best opportunity for success. It had two concentric rings, supporting 259 screens. The larger size would better justify advertising and the Circle's other expenses, and the large population base could be enough to fill all those slots.

Unfortunately, Smith's bad timing hit again. In 1963, Albuquerque was going through something of a drive-in theater glut, with 10 others competing against the Circle. Newspaper ads reflected a ticket price war, a race to the bottom for income. The Circle closed after one season.

Although he didn't use the word "privacy," it was implied when Smith told *Boxoffice* about the difference in

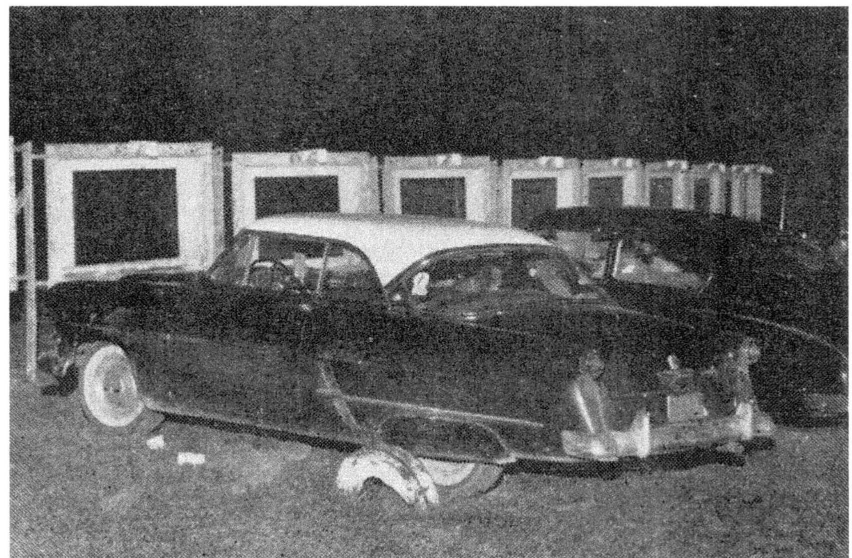

Cars at the Autoscope parked very close to the screen, as shown in this photo from *Boxoffice* magazine.

the viewing experience. "Its individual screens give an 'exclusive' feeling to the patron," he said, "the same personal impact that the individual speakers had when they were introduced." That was an important factor in what became the most successful Autoscope, the Mini Drive-In in Joplin MO.

In those days before the internet or even home video, if a fan of *Marital Fulfillment* or *Captain Lust* wanted to view that movie, he had to find a theater showing it. The Mini's tiny screens prevented neighbors or anyone driving by from watching. Its hardcore fans kept the

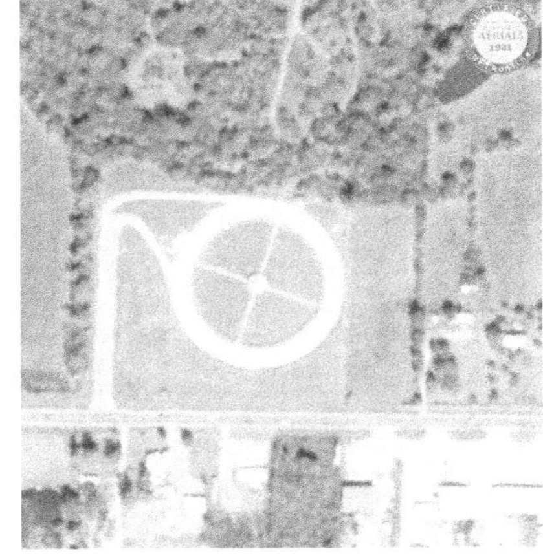

Joplin MO's Autoscope, called the Mini Drive-In, was still operating in this 1981 photo. © HistoricAerials.com, used by permission.

drive-in alive from 1971 through about 1985. The Mini's remains, mainly the central projection building, are still in a wooded field today.

The Autoscope concept limped along elsewhere for a few more years. In 1973, a company called U.S. TRAD said that eight Autoscopes had been built. That matches the total I know about – the four above plus Anchorage AK, Houston TX, Richland WA, and Springdale AR. The company said 15 more would open that year, but I don't think that ever happened. The Autoscope was an invention in search of a purpose, and the purpose it eventually found is long gone.

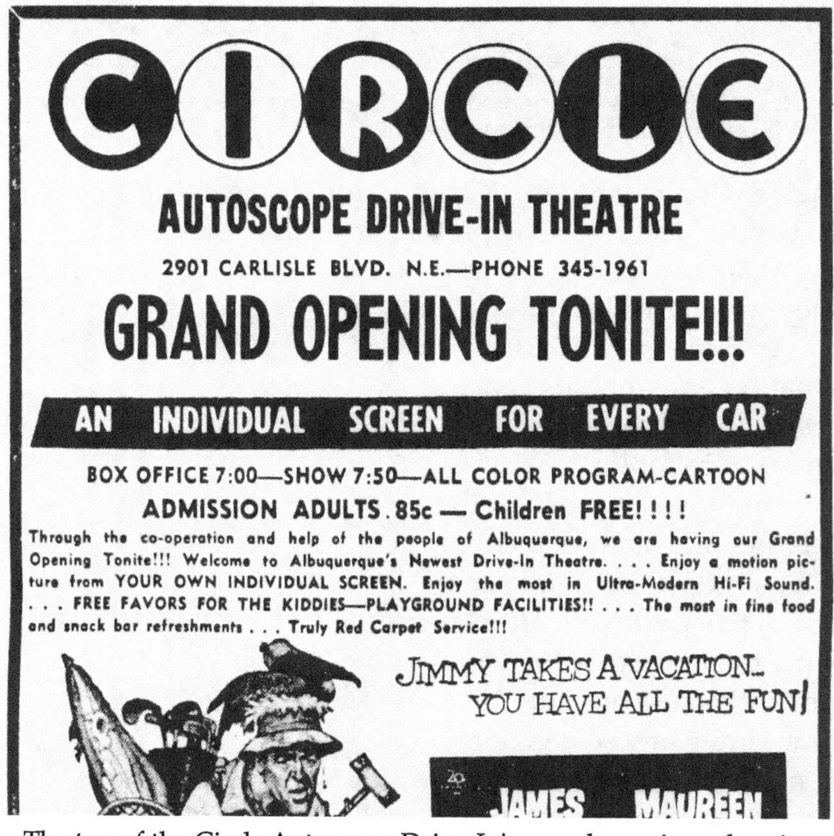

The top of the Circle Autoscope Drive-In's grand opening ad, as it appeared in the *Albuquerque Tribune*.

Belen

A group of Spanish colonists founded Nuestra Señora de Belén (Our Lady of Bethlehem) in 1740. A few decades later, Spain built a fort to protect the site. The city's modern history began in 1880 when the Atchison, Topeka & Santa Fe Railway showed up, and ramped up after 1907 with the completion of the Belen Cutoff, which allowed freight trains to bypass the steep grades of Raton Pass.

Zia Drive-In

Location: Over a mile north of town on US 85
Opened: Oct. 24, 1951
Closed: 1969?
Capacity: 250 cars

I'm sorry to say that I know almost nothing about the Zia, a condition that would be corrected if I could find more local newspapers from the period when it was open. In October 1951, *Motion Picture Daily* reported that Theatre Enterprises of Dallas was building a drive-in in Belen, and that it could begin operating that fall. The 1952 *Theatre Catalog*, published early that year, included the Zia, owned by Theatre Enterprises, with a capacity of 250 cars.

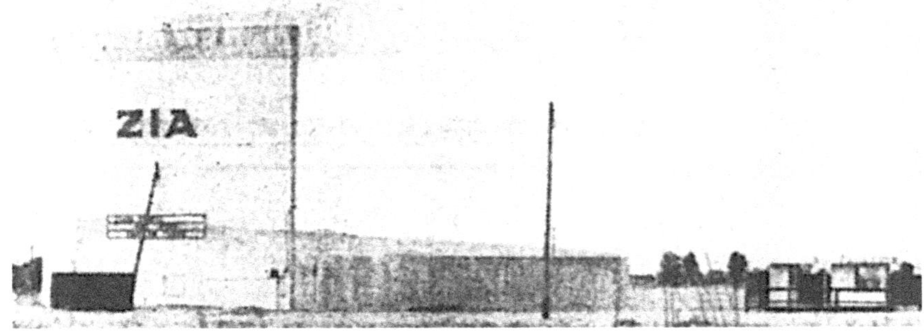

The *Belen News-Bulletin* published this photo of the Zia's screen tower the day after it opened.

Frontier Theatres had taken over the Zia by 1966, when the *Motion Picture Almanac* listed its capacity at 197. The following year, Zia manager Richard Hugg was one of the attendees at a Frontier meeting. Common-wealth bought out Frontier in 1968, and in April 1969, it

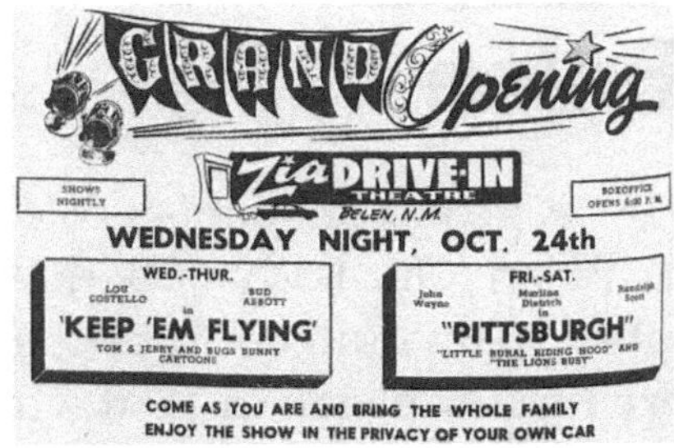

The Zia's grand opening ad as it appeared two days earlier in the *Belen News-Bulletin*.

sold the Zia along with Belen's indoor Oñate to Gilbert Tabet. (Tabet also founded the Circle T Drive-In, a Belen restaurant that's still there today. But I digress.) Subsequent stories in *Boxoffice* indicated that Tabet was renovating the Oñate but didn't mention the Zia. A 1971 aerial photo showed the drive-in site had been razed; today it's home to the Belen Flea Market.

Carlsbad

After growing up in "the Cave State" (Missouri) and having toured at least a dozen caves, I was still blown away by Carlsbad Caverns National Park. It's so huge, so historic, so much of a must-see. Another tourist attraction on the other side of Carlsbad is the Pecos River Plume, an aqueduct that crosses the river to deliver its irrigation water.

For three weeks in August 1946, something called the "Lazy H Corral Drive-In Pitcher Show / Just this side of White's City" advertised in the *Carlsbad Current-Argus*. That sounds like a bedsheet-and-loudspeaker, makeshift kind of drive-in, and it's the only mention I've ever seen of it. With no "permanent" predecessors, the Lazy H might have been the state's first drive-in theater, so I had to include it somewhere here under Carlsbad.

Big Sky Drive-In

Location: South of town, west of the intersection of US 62/285 and Center Avenue
Opened: June 28, 1960
Closed: Oct. 26, 1979?
Capacity: 700 cars

In January 1956, *Boxoffice* reported that Owen "O. O." Knotts from Hobbs had started construction of an 800-car drive-in on the Cavern highway south of Carlsbad. There were never any follow-up reports, but the project sounds so similar to the eventual Big Sky that I wonder whether any of its work was part of the final product four years later.

In 1960, Charles C. "Charley" Wolfe was a vice president and general manager of Tom Griffing's All States Theatres, so he knew how to build and run a drive-in theater. That year, he left Abilene TX to build and operate his own drive-in in Carlsbad. When he broke ground in March, the theater was going to be called the Cavemen Drive-In, after the Carlsbad High School's sports nickname. He soon changed his mind; in less than two months, he was calling the unfinished project the Big Sky.

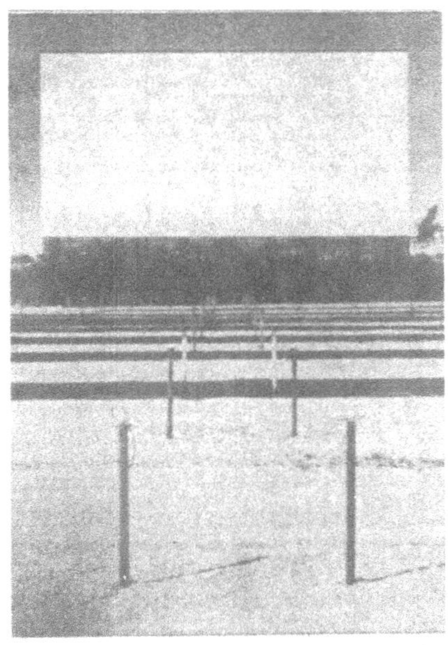

The Big Sky included this photo of its wide, modern screen in the middle of its grand opening ad in the *Carlsbad Current-Argus*.

Construction took longer than expected because the site Wolfe chose turned out to be solid rock under a thin layer of dirt. It took over a ton of dynamite to level the drive-in's parking area and prepare a foundation for its 40-foot screen tower.

On the Big Sky's opening night, hundreds of cars lined up for a half mile along South Canal Street waiting to get in, blocking the entrances to the motels along the way. The *Carlsbad Current-Argus* called it "by far the biggest theatre opening in the city's history."

In the fall of 1963, Wolfe sold the Big Sky to Frontier Theaters, which already owned three other Carlsbad theaters – the Fiesta Drive-In and the indoor Caverns and Cactus. In April 1967, 60-mile-per-hour winds blew down part of the Big Sky's screen. Winds damaged the screen twice more in 1977.

In 1979, years after Commonwealth bought out Frontier, the Big Sky ran its final ads in the *Current-Argus*. In April 1983, the city announced that it would work with Commonwealth to tear down its screen tower, which had "been in disrepair for several years and is considered an 'eyesore' by the State Highway Department." A Walmart occupies the site today.

Corral Drive-In

Location: About two miles northwest of town on US 285
Opened: April 13, 1952
Closed: Sept. 2, 1957
Capacity: 256 cars

Ray Bartlett of nearby Artesia was the city (regional?) supervisor for Theater Enterprises. He also owned his own theaters in Artesia. I'm fuzzy on the ownership structure; it's possible he and the company both owned a piece of "his" theaters. Anyway, Theater Enterprises' indoor Corral in Carlsbad closed in 1951, and that prompted the company to build the Corral Drive-In "opposite the old CCC camp" between the two cities.

It amuses me, and illustrates the fallibility of memory, that two retrospectives got the Corral's closing date wrong. An Associated Press story in 1998, carried in the *Alamogordo Daily News* among others, said that the

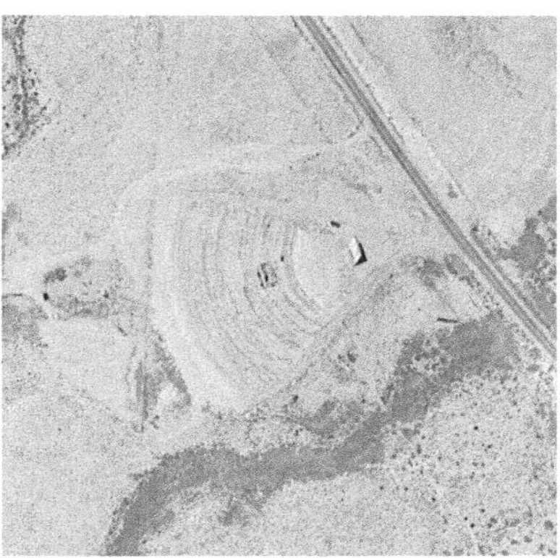

When the New Mexico Department of Transportation took this photo in April 1965, the Corral had been closed for over seven years.

Corral, forgotten by most Carlsbad residents, "opened in 1952 and closed two years later." Even the *Carlsbad Current-Argus*, writing about Ray Bartlett's son Bill in 2008, wrote that the Corral closed in 1955.

In fact, the Corral's relatively uneventful life lasted six seasons. Its final ad on Sept. 1, 1957 in the *Current-Argus* stated that it was closing for the season on Labor Day. The Corral never reopened. A Lowe's hardware store occupies the site today.

Fiesta Drive-In

Location: On the south side of town, a couple of blocks west of US 285 on Fiesta Drive
Opened: Aug. 10, 1948
Closed: Dec. 9, 2018
Capacity: 600 cars

The Fiesta Drive-In lived two lives, one as the first to open in Carlsbad and the other as the last to close.

Carl Burton from Oklahoma City bought 18 acres on the south side of Carlsbad and started building in early

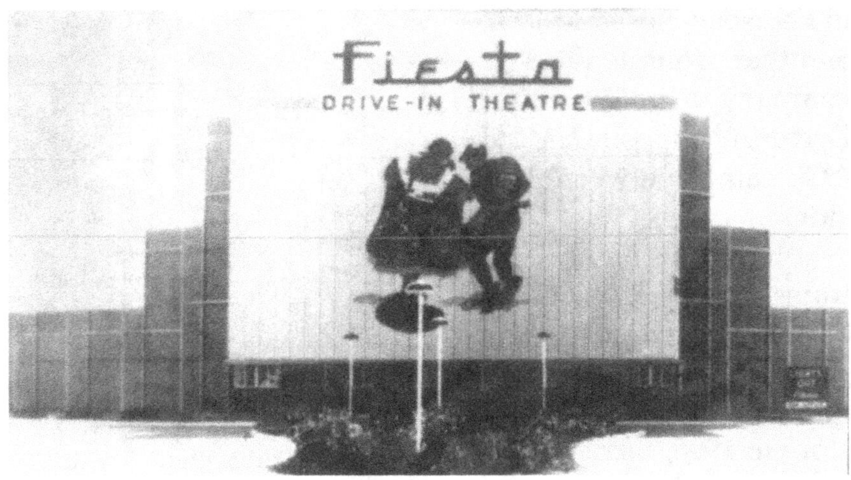

This photo of the original Fiesta Drive-In screen tower ran as part of an *Carlsbad Current-Argus* ad celebrating the rebirth of the Fiesta as a modern, three-screen drive-in.

1948. The screen tower was to be 54 feet high, and the drive-in would include a snack bar and playground. "This is a lazy man's paradise," Burton said. "You don't have to leave your car. You drive in to the site and buy your ticket. Waitresses will come to your car so that you can order refreshments." (Although the Fiesta briefly offered car hop service, a later owner recalled that it didn't last long.)

Less than a week before the Fiesta opened, Burton sold it to local theater man Ray Bartlett. Burton would later build the 22 Drive-In in Fort Smith AR and the Riverside in Little Rock.

The new drive-in was gorgeous. Its screen tower featured "the largest animated, neonized mural (of a Mexican hat dance) to be found between Los Angeles and Dallas and south of Denver," according to the *Carlsbad Current-Argus*. Its entrance was lined with "large, multi-colored zinnias, moss, roses, and shrubbery."

One night in 1951, a family from California fell asleep during the movies at the Fiesta and woke to find that the gates had been locked. They were unable to leave until a

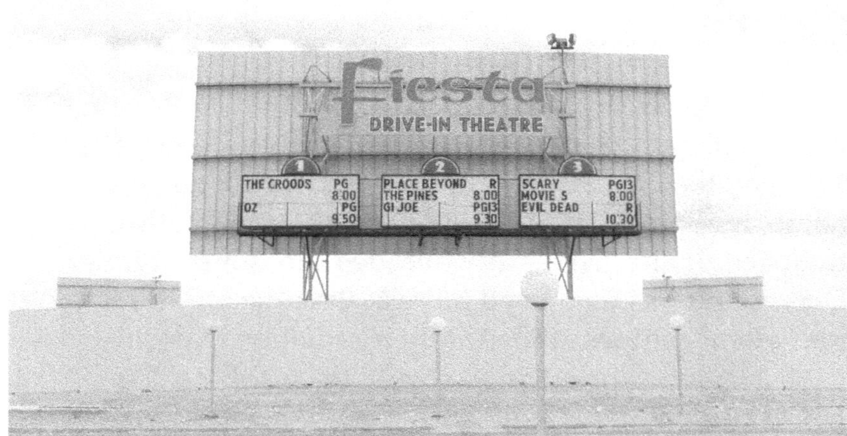

The newer Fiesta was a drive-in done right. Its modern screens and equipment could have lasted for decades, if only its builder hadn't passed away. 2013 photo by the author.

caretaker arrived at 7 the next morning. In 1955, a fire broke out in the small apartment at the base of the screen tower, but it was extinguished before it could spread to the main structure.

The Fiesta's owners expanded and refurbished it in 1960, including a new refreshment center building. At some point, Frontier Theaters bought the drive-in. The Fiesta ended its first life on Aug. 16, 1970, when it ran its final ad in the *Current-Argus*. The screen tower was demolished in 1983.

In 1990, the Fiesta's second life began when local entrepreneur Brad Light rebuilt and reopened it as a modern three-screen drive-in with FM radio sound. Brad ran the whole show until a few months before he passed away in 2010. His son Sidney Light took up the helm, partly to maintain his father's legacy. After running the drive-in for several years, Sidney sold it in December 2018. The site was razed for a small industrial park, but its name lives on as Fiesta Drive.

Carrizozo

Carrizozo, the seat of Lincoln County, was the first municipality to be dusted with radioactive fallout. The Trinity Site, where the US detonated the first nuclear bomb, is about 35 miles west of town. Although the radioactivity decayed away decades ago, some "Trinity Downwinders" who lived there at the time are still hoping for federal compensation for their radiation exposure.

Nike Drive-In

Location: On the northwest side of town on US 380, less than a mile from its intersection with US 54
Opened: June 22, 1956
Closed: Sept. 27, 1964
Capacity: 200 cars

The Nike opened on June 22, 1956, built by Mr. and Mrs. Bill Skelton. Fred Miller leased the drive-in in September 1961, then Doug and Betty Williams leased it for the 1962 season. Robert (Bob) Means ran the Nike in 1963, and Bill Baker opened it for its final season in 1964. It closed on Sunday, Sept. 27, with a showing of *Captain Newman, M.D.* starring Gregory Peck and Tony Curtis.

The Nike's sign survived until July 1967, when a 15-year-old ran his car into it. Means bought the site from Skelton in 1969, planning to develop it as a trailer park; he said he'd

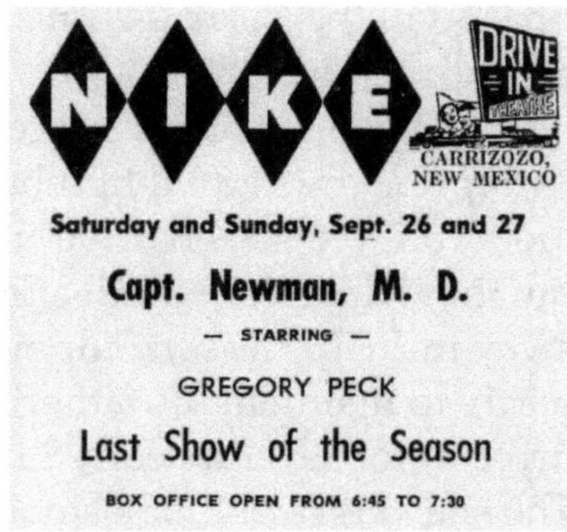

The Nike's final ad in the *Lincoln County News.*

keep the concession/projection building to use as a utility room. Means sold the screen for scrap in 1975, and it came down on Feb. 10 of that year. At the time, Means said the Nike had closed in 1961, illustrating the unreliable nature of memory, even of a business that one had operated just 12 years earlier. But I digress.

The *Albuquerque Journal* wrote in 1996 that a 75-year-old former cowboy was living in the Nike's old projection room. That building is still there today, surrounded by old cars and trucks.

Chama

The Cumbres and Toltec Scenic Railroad, a narrow-gauge route that crosses back and forth 11 times between New Mexico and Colorado each trip, runs from Antonito CO to Chama. The region has hosted several Hollywood film shoots, including *The Cowboys* (1972), *Indiana Jones and the Last Crusade* (1989), and *A Million Ways to Die in the West* (2014).

Kelly's / Rainbow / Chama Drive-In

Location: On US 64/84E, less than a half mile west of its intersection with NM 17
Opened: 1960?
~~**Closed:** 1985?~~ active
Capacity: 200? cars

The drive-in in Chama is operating again today, yet its vague history makes it seem mysterious from my distant perspective. Its story probably starts with Mike Kelly, who ran Chama's indoor Rainbow Theatre (at least) by the mid-1950s. At some point, Kelly built or bought a small drive-in. A YouTube video by Roger Hogan said that the drive-in opened in 1960, which sounds about right. It was definitely built by October 1961, when the state Department of Transportation shot an aerial photo that included the drive-in.

One of the few newspaper clippings I could find, from the local *Nora News* on June 24, 1968, included an ad for the Rainbow Drive-In. It was not unusual for a theater owner to seasonally close the local indoor theater and move personnel and equipment to open the drive-in during the warmer summer months. It sounds like that's what happened here.

Boxoffice articles reported that Kelly celebrated his 35th year in the movie business in 1968, and in October 1969, he said he wouldn't reopen the indoor Rainbow "for the winter, as he has done in the past." Kelly passed away in May 1978; his obituary said he had "operated the Rainbow Theatre and the Chama Drive-In in Chama, N.M., up until the time of his retirement from the business some years ago." Hogan's video said that the drive-in closed in 1985.

Chama's drive-in never showed up on any of the industry's lists. The first I heard of it was *Albuquerque Journal* columnist Toby Smith's sidebar from Aug. 11, 1996, talking about closed New Mexico drive-ins. "One drive-in, in Chama," he wrote, "called itself Kelly's, after the resident who owned it". That's the only reference I've ever seen to that name, but Smith must have found it somewhere.

When I went looking for the drive-in's exact location, I found that not only was it intact, it was active, sort of. Local businesses have sponsored occasional shows for at least a couple of years, and now an organization called "Elevate Chama" is in charge. I'm happy that it's alive now, but I wish I knew more about this drive-in's beginnings.

Clayton

The downtown Luna Theater has entertained Clayton movie fans for over a century. In 1916, German immigrant Morris Herzstein opened the Mission Theater, which had a ballroom in its basement. Gibraltar Enterprises, a loose coalition of small regional theater owners, bought the Mission in 1935 and remodeled it into the Luna, complete with a winking neon moon face on its sign.

Trail Drive-In

Location: Over two miles southeast of town on US 87
Opened: June? 1952
Closed: 1985?
Capacity: 350 cars

Hubbard & Murphy Theatres, which operated indoor theaters in Clayton and Raton, announced in January 1950 that it was going to build a drive-in in Clayton similar to the Ski-Hi it was finishing in Alamosa CO. Although *Boxoffice* later included the then-unnamed Clayton drive-in in its 1950 and 1951 lists, I'll bet it was delayed by building material restrictions prompted by the Korean War.

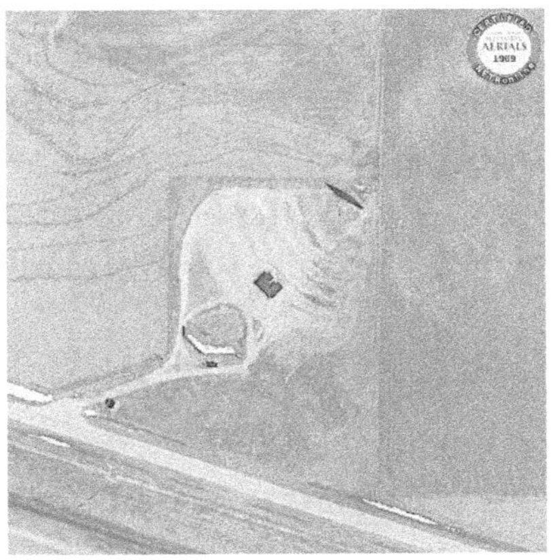

The Trail's driveway was angled west towards Clayton, as seen in this 1969 photo. © HistoricAerials.com, used by permission.

The first real note came in the July 5, 1952 issue of *Motion Picture Herald*, which wrote, "Tom Murphy has opened his new 330-car drive-in, the Trail, at Clayton, N. M. It is being managed by his brother, William Murphy."

I'm sad to say that's about all I know for sure about the Trail, except that it probably hung around for a long time. In his 2018 book *Historic Movie Theatres of New Mexico*, Jeff Berg wrote that the Trail closed in 1985. The *Motion Picture Almanac* included it annually through its final drive-in list in the 1988 edition, still owned by Murphy. However, the *MPA* was known to be slow to notice closures.

A 1997 aerial photo showed the screen intact, but a note in the May 7, 2000 *Albuquerque Journal* listed the Trail as defunct. Today the screen is gone, but the concession building and speaker poles still stand.

Clovis

In addition to Cannon Air Force Base, which brought a lot of patrons to the city's drive-ins, Clovis was home to Norman Petty's recording studio. Beginning in the late 1950s, Petty's "Clovis sound" of rockabilly cranked out hits such as "That'll be the Day," "Peggy Sue," "Ooby Dooby," and "Sugar Shack." The Norman and Vi Petty Rock & Roll Museum is open to visitors, and the original studio one mile west is available for tours by appointment.

Comet Drive-In

Location: On the west side of town on US 60/84, just east of Mission Garden Cemetery
Opened: Aug. 22, 1958
Closed: May 15, 1960
Capacity: 546 cars

The Comet had a very short life. It looks like its screen was built over a year before the drive-in opened. A

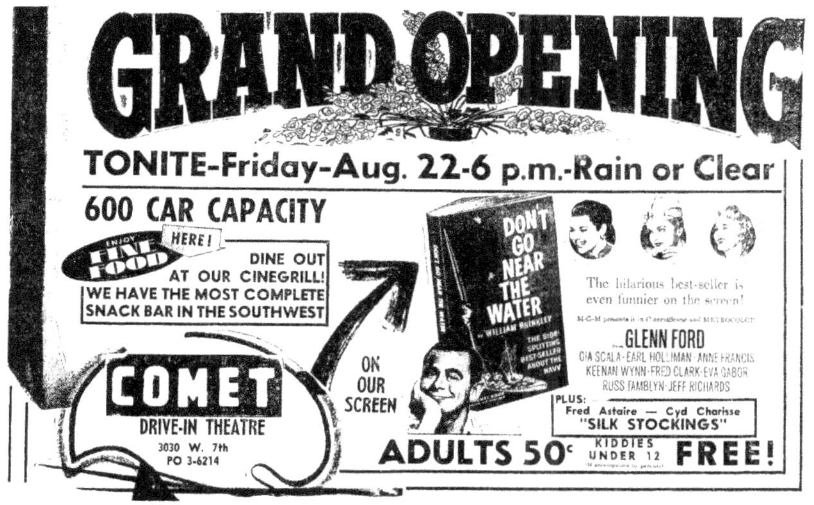

The Comet's grand opening ad in the *Clovis News-Journal*. "Cinegrill" was a nice turn of phrase, wasn't it?

newspaper ad in February 1957 described a nursery's location as three blocks north of the "Comet Drive Inn Screen on West 7th." A December 1957 ad for residential lots also used the unopened Comet Drive-In as a landmark.

W. O. Bearden and local man Loyd Franklin, owners of Clovis's other drive-ins, built the Comet with double ramps to fit more cars on the lot. The screen tower was 85x65 feet.

Less than two years after the Comet opened, the La Fonda's screen went up in flames. Franklin shut down the Comet and planned to move its screen to replace the La Fonda's. However, in the process of preparing it for transport, the 35-ton Comet screen fell over. No one was hurt, but the screen was in such bad shape that Franklin had to build a new one. The Comet never reopened; its former concession stand now sits alone on a flat vacant lot.

Four-Lane Drive-In

Location: Five miles east of town on US 60/70/84, two miles west of Texico
    Opened: May 12, 1950
    Closed: Nov. 21, 1954
    Capacity: 444 cars

John and Evelyn Whipple of Clovis partnered with Kansas City MO theater owners Myron and Betty Finkelstein combined to build the area's second drive-in on the four-lane highway to Texico. It was actually closer to the Texas border than to Clovis. Construction took four months, and the Four-Lane opened with a refreshment bar and a children's playground complete "with a competent lady attendant."

A high school student at the time who worked at the Four-Lane said it was popularly known as Whipple's Theater. The drive-in's screen collapsed in an April 1951 windstorm, but Whipple rebuilt it.

During the drive-in's off-seasons, Whipple worked as a service manager at the Montgomery Ward in Clovis. After the 1953 season, he opened a business in Texico and advertised free demonstrations of home-installed television through a truck-mounted aerial. I think that

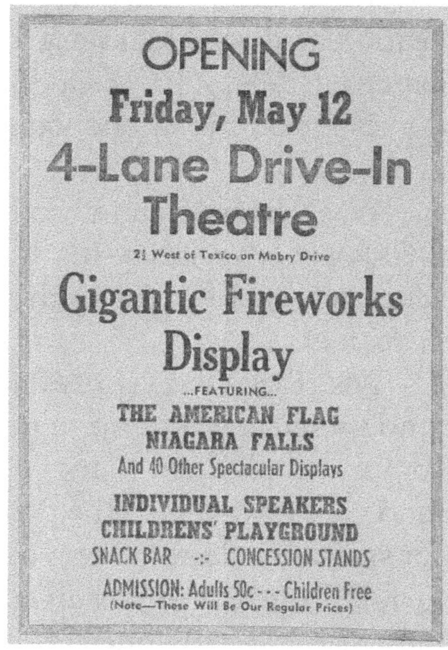

The Four-Lane (or 4-Lane) advertised its grand opening in the *State Line Tribune* of Farwell TX, just across the border.

was a signal that Whipple saw more folks interested in TV than in movies. The Four-Lane quietly closed at the end of the 1954 season.

In 1956, two men were arrested for stealing copper wire from the Four-Lane site. Around 1958, the owners of Clovis's other drive-ins, W. O. Bearden and Loyd Franklin, bought the Four-Lane and sold it to Stuckey's, which built one of its famous roadside restaurants there. Today, the site is home to a marijuana dispensary, coyly named Stickey's.

La Fonda Drive-In

Location: Just north of town on New Mexico 18
Opened: July 4, 1952
Closed: Oct. 3, 1981
Capacity: 400 cars

Regional drive-in entrepreneur Wendell Oren "W. O." Bearden teamed up with local theater owner Loyd Franklin to build Clovis' third drive-in in 1952. The back of the La Fonda's screen tower featured a western desert mural with cowboys and a chuck wagon.

The most memorable night of the La Fonda's life was on Friday, Aug. 14, 1959. While movie patrons were watching a show, the 85-foot screen tower caught fire, and the flames were soon visible for miles.

In the aftermath, Franklin planned to replace the burnt screen with the one built just a couple of years earlier at the

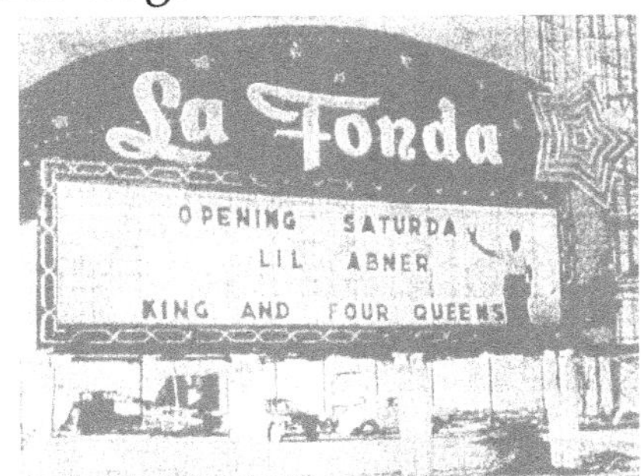

That's La Fonda co-owner Loyd Franklin posing in front of the La Fonda marquee. This photo was published by the *Clovis News-Journal* just before the drive-in reopened with a new screen in 1960.

neighboring Comet Drive-In. As workers were taking it down for transport, the Comet's screen broke. The owners had to build a new screen instead, and the La Fonda reopened in July 1960.

The drive-in moved a mile north of its original location in the summer of 1974. The newer location featured radio sound, and in December, it added a second screen.

In April 1979, Franklin retired and leased the La Fonda to Commonwealth Theatres for five years with an option to buy. Commonwealth ran it for just three years, closing the city's last drive-in on the first Saturday in October 1981. Its screens were dismantled in 1985, and a Lowe's hardware store occupies the site today.

Yucca Drive-In

Location: About 1½ miles south of town on US 70
Opened: July 1948
Closed: Dec. 3, 1978
Capacity: 400 cars

Clovis' first drive-in theater went through a lot of owners in its first 12 months. It started with three, John Sands, W. M. Goates and John Blocker, all of Plainview, TX. They built the Yucca, which opened in mid-July 1948. By September, they had sold the Yucca to Charles Wolfe. In April 1949, new owner Tom Griffing sold the drive-in to Russell

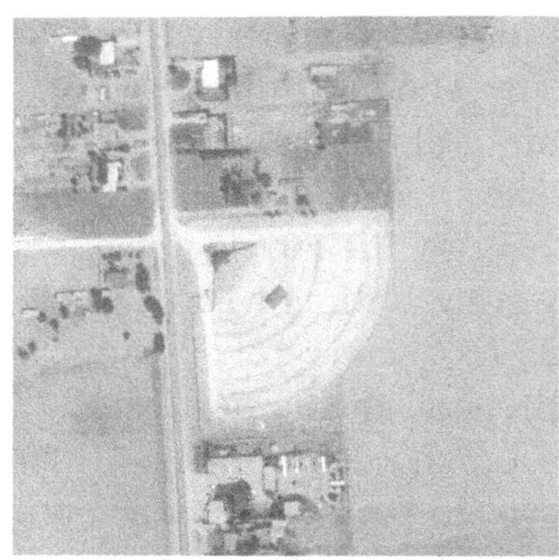

The Yucca sat next to scattered farmhouses, according to this 1962 photo taken by the New Mexico Department of Transportation.

Hardwick, who owned the indoor Lyceum and State theaters in Clovis.

Less than two years after it opened, the Yucca saw major renovations for the 1950 season, including a new patio with chairs and tables, enlarged snack bar, bigger rest rooms, a new projection booth, new sound system and rebuilt ramps. By 1952, it was owned by Theatre Enterprises of Dallas.

The Yucca finally found its permanent owner in 1954 when the builders of the La Fonda, W. O. Bearden and Loyd Franklin, bought the last of their competitors. It spent the next 25 years fairly quietly. When Franklin retired in early 1979, he sold the Yucca to Carl Deaton on the condition that it not reopen as a theater. The site is mostly vacant today, with hints of the former ramps still visible.

Cuba

This small village, nestled against the Sierra Nacimiento on the border of the Santa Fe National Forest, is about halfway between Albuquerque and Farmington on the four-lane US 550. Cuba apparently hosted the last drive-in to be built in New Mexico in the 20th Century.

Placita Hills Drive-In

Location: About 1½ miles south of town on then-New Mexico 44
Opened: 1979?
Closed: 1987?
Capacity: 200 cars

I'm sad to say that I've got almost nothing about the Placita Hills. Its first appearance in the annual *Motion Picture Almanac* drive-in list was in the 1980 edition, which listed the owner as W. Edge, and the capacity as 200. Its final appearance, with the same information, was in the 1982 edition.

Aerial photos show empty land at the site in 1977, an intact drive-in in 1981, 1982 and 1987, and the screen missing by 1996. Today, a marijuana company sits between old Highway 44 and the former Placita Hills' viewing field.

From notes passed to me by the current occupants, it sounds like there was an indoor theater adjacent to the drive-in. The aerial photos suggest that the drive-in came first, but they might have been built almost simultaneously.

That's it. If you know anything else about this drive-in, please drop me a line.

Deming

The golden spike marked the ceremonial completion of the first US transcontinental railroad in 1869 near Omaha NE. The silver spike, for second place, was installed in Deming in 1881, connecting the Southern Pacific with a subsidiary of the Atchison, Topeka & Santa Fe railroad.

Mimbres Drive-In

Location: About a mile east of town on then-US 70/80/180
Opened: Oct. 10, 1951
Closed: 1984?
Capacity: 300 cars

Local theater man George Dowdle partnered with Theatre Enterprises to build Deming's only drive-in. They announced the project in July 1950, but the project was delayed, probably by the Korean War-inspired building material restrictions, until late 1951. The original plans called for 400 cars, but the Mimbres accommodated only about half that number when it opened.

R. I. Payne of Theatre Enterprises was listed as the owner in 1952. Before the season started that year, the drive-in's ramps were graveled for "all-weather service with no shut down because of rain," according to manager Alvah Haley.

By 1963, Frontier Theaters had stepped in as the Mimbres' owner. In 1968, Commonwealth Theaters bought out Frontier. For

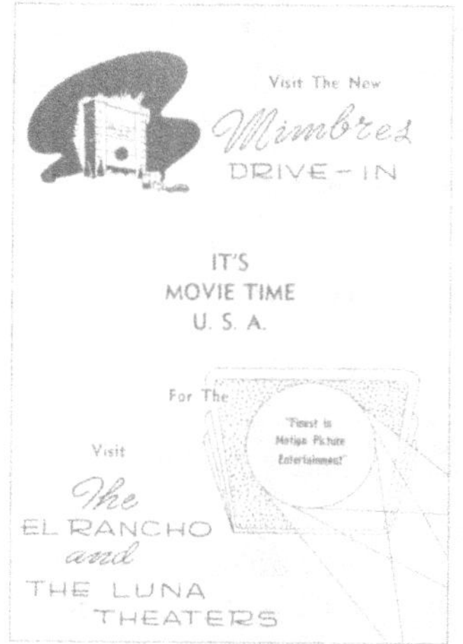

The Mimbres Drive-In and the other local theaters advertised in the 1952 edition of *The Wildcat*, the Deming High School yearbook.

the 1971 season opener, Commonwealth celebrated its wider screen and "about 300" first-class speakers with a Miss Mimbres Drive-In contest.

In September 1976, a Deming teenager working as the Mimbres' manager was arrested there and later pleaded guilty to possessing a bit of hashish and marijuana. He lost his job.

The exact closing date for the Mimbres is fuzzy. It definitely opened for the season in April 1981, but by June, it had ceased running ads in the *Deming Headlight*. In 1982, it co-sponsored the local Great American Duck Race. When Les Dollison was elected president of the New Mexico Theatre Association in October 1982, the *Headlight* mentioned that he owned the Mimbres.

I believe the Mimbres operated through 1984. A *Headlight* classified ad on July 4, 1984, offering the drive-in for sale, said that the site was "Presently a Drive-In Theater." And a *Washington Post* travel column on Dec. 16,

1984 wrote, "The Mimbres Drive-In shows PG classics. Can there be any other drive-in surviving on PG?"

The drive-in was definitely closed by August 1985, when Luna County commissioners approved a fundraiser "at the old Mimbres". The words "Gone With the Wind" were written on its wall by 1986, and in October that year, the screen came down. An RV Park occupies the site today.

Española

Northern New Mexico College is based in Española, about 25 miles north of Santa Fe. It started in El Rito NM in 1909 as the Spanish American Normal School, the first Hispanic-serving college in the United States. Northern came to Española in 1971, where it expanded to a community college, then a teachers college, then a fairly typical college, offering a wide variety of 50 certificates and degrees.

Chico / Starlighter Drive-In

Location: North of town on then-US 64, now Riverside Drive
Opened: April 28, 1950
Closed: September 25, 1994
Capacity: 373 cars

Fidel Theatres, which owned the local indoor houses, built and opened Española's only drive-in, the Chico, in early 1950. Fidel sold the Chico to Mr. and Mrs. L. H. Mills in August 1954, and again to Lester Dollison in April 1957. I'll bet the Mills couple was paying installments and allowed Fidel to reclaim the Chico. Between sales, somebody widened the Chico's screen in 1956.

In June 1960, a teen roofer working on the Chico's roof was struck and killed by lightning.

Dollison, who owned a bunch of New Mexico theaters, made one of his favorite moves before the 1962 season. He renamed the drive-in the Starlighter, and knowing Dollison, that was probably after a local name-the-theater contest.

In September 1979, a dispute between two groups culminated in the shooting death at the Starlighter's gate of one of the young men in one of the groups. A 26-year-old was arrested and later found guilty of second-degree murder and aggravated assault.

The Ohkay Owingeh Pueblo, a Native American

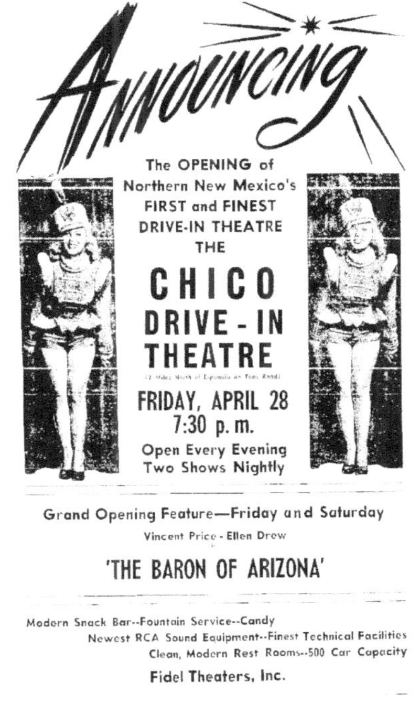

The top part of the Chico's grand opening ad, as it appeared in the *Santa Fe New Mexican*.

community known at the time as San Juan Pueblo, asserted a claim over part of the Starlighter's property in 1980. It had the right-of-way to an abandoned highway about 35 feet wide that split the drive-in's land. Dollison signed a lease with the pueblo that year.

Valentin Leyba Jr., who had been managing the Starlighter since the late 1960s, bought it from Dollison's company in a lease-purchase deal in 1982. In the summer of 1986, the pueblo fenced off one of the drive-in's entrances and part of its viewing field, claiming that no one had made the lease payments due that January. In December 1986, Dollison's company filed an eviction request to remove Leyba from the Starlighter site. The drive-in was closed for the next two seasons.

Carl Kahn's Blue Pear Corporation, soon to merge with the Trans-Lux theater chain, bought the Starlighter in August 1988. They reopened it the following spring after refurbishing with new equipment and radio sound. Despite the changes, the Starlighter was not a success. After being listed for sale during most of 1994, the site was sold to a residential developer in February 1995, and a demolition crew tore down its screen two months later. Today a tire store sits on the drive-in's former entrance road, and its viewing field is filled with houses.

Eunice

This small city in the southeastern corner of the state is home to the Eunice High School Cardinals, which has won more New Mexico baseball state championships than any other team. Its 18 wins (as of this writing), starting in 1960, include the 2022 championship, when the team won the 2A title, finishing with a 26-1 record.

Star Drive-In

Location: Just west of town on New Mexico 176
Opened: January? 1952
Closed: 1974?
Capacity: 400 cars

Sorry, but I don't have much about the Star. The drive-in's first ad in the *Hobbs Daily News-Sun* was on January 20, 1952, but it didn't say anything about a grand opening. The 1952 *Theatre Catalog* listed its owner as O. O. Knotts. (That would be Owen Knotts, who later built the Sunset and the Trade Wind in Hobbs.) In January 1955, *Motion Picture Exhibitor* wrote that the Star's owner, C. C. Caldwell, had installed CinemaScope. Mr. Caldwell's obituary in the April 10, 1968 *News-Sun* said that he owned and operated the Star.

And I know even less about when the drive-in closed. A Star Drive-In restaurant opened in Hobbs by the 1970s, confusing the issue. In April 1974, a short *News-Sun* bio for Lea County Magistrate candidate Lesta D. Burdett said that he "operates the Star Drive-In Theatre." A 1983 aerial photo showed the drive-in long gone. An oil and gas field support service company occupies the site today.

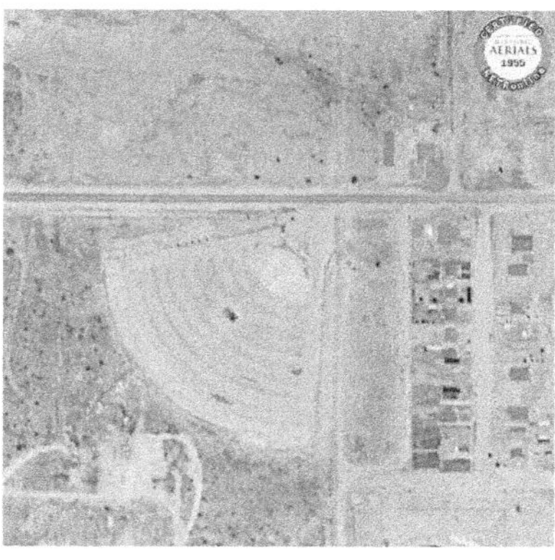

The Star in 1955. © Historic-Aerials.com, used by permission.

Farmington

Farmington spent the first few decades of the 1900s as a fruit and farm hub. Then the San Juan Basin Natural Gas Pipeline was built in 1953, and the city's population grew from less than 4000 in 1950 to over 23,000 in 1960. Six drive-ins opened in the region during that decade, though only three of them were within Farmington itself.

Also see: Aztec, Shiprock, Spencerville.

Apache Drive-In

Location: On the west side of town between US 550 and Apache Road

Opened: May 29, 1952
Closed: Aug. 19, 2001
Capacity: 750 cars

The Allen family, owners of most of Farmington's indoor theaters, reacted to the new drive-in competition

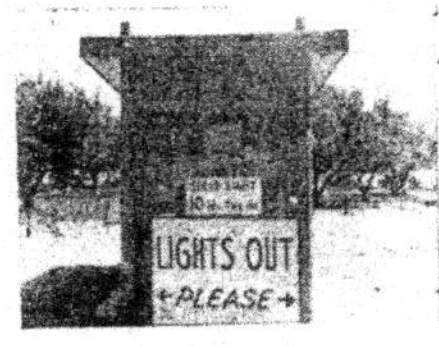

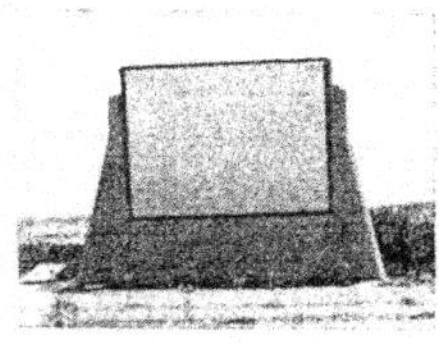

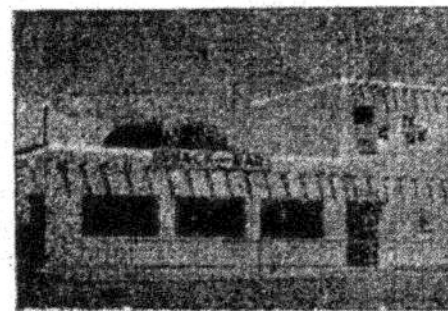

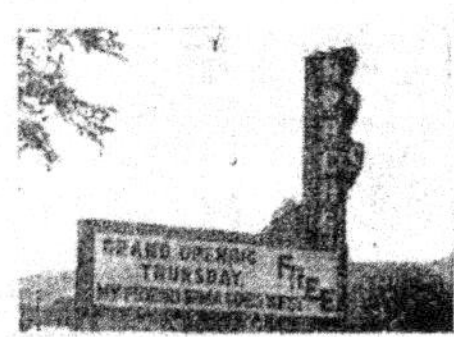

This section of the Apache's grand opening ad, from the *Farmington Daily Times*, includes several glimpses of its appearance.

and the region's oil-driven population boom by building their own drive-in. At that point, the theater dynasty was headed by Russell Allen and his nephew, Kelly Crawford.

The winning entry of a countywide naming contest for the drive-in was the Apache, based on its location on Apache Road, also known then as the Shiprock highway. My favorite feature was its children's playground, built in an old apple orchard. The owners removed only enough trees to accommodate the swings and teeter-totters.

Allen and Crawford must have felt the same about their pastoral playground. In 1957, when they decided to add a second screen to meet growing demand, they built the second field at a right angle to the first in order to spare the playground just behind the projection building.

The Apache's first screen was 35x80 feet; the newer one was 40x90. Their fields were fenced with two-inch steel piping painted yellow and lit with army surplus red, white, and blue airport runway lights. The owners added an arrow with the word "Twin" to the marquee. Local author Zang Wood later wrote, "The whole community agreed they cooked absolutely the best tasting hamburgers and cheeseburgers that any were privileged to eat."

In all, the Apache lasted for 50 seasons, much longer than most drive-ins. In 2000, when the *Albuquerque Journal* included it as one of the four active drive-ins in the state, it had switched to FM radio sound but was still owned by members of

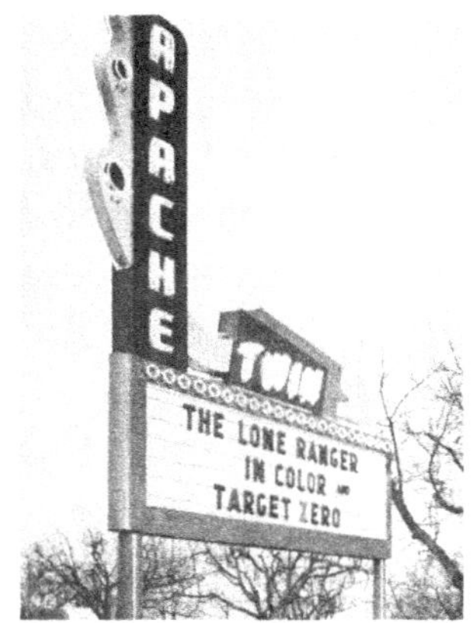

The Apache sign with the "Twin" added, as it appeared in a 1958 issue of *Boxoffice*.

the same family – Lane Allen, Larry Allen, and Evelyn Crawford. The Apache's final ad in the *Farmington Daily Times* came in August 2001, and the site was advertised for sale in March 2002. A Walmart went up a few years later, and that's still what's there today.

Mesa Drive-In

Location: About three miles southeast of town on then-New Mexico 17, now US 64
   Opened: May 30, 1950
   Closed: Aug. 22, 1955
   Capacity: 400 cars

Frank Budai, who had moved from Cincinnati OH to the small San Juan River valley community of Waterflow, began building the region's first drive-in theater in the spring of 1950. He hired a driller to sink a well for a water supply but hit oil instead. Still looking for water, Budai reached out to Tom Kerby, who had a farm with a well on the other side of the highway. Kerby ran a one-inch pipe through a culvert under the road to the future Mesa site.

The Mesa's 100-foot screen tower was built of concrete and Oregon pine. Budai managed the drive-in, and Edward Pierce was the projectionist when it opened.

In his booklet *Sodas & Shows*, Zang Wood wrote that Budai leased the Mesa to "an unknown party" in late 1954, but the *Farmington Daily Times* wrote in July 1955 that Budai still owned and operated the drive-in. Whoever was

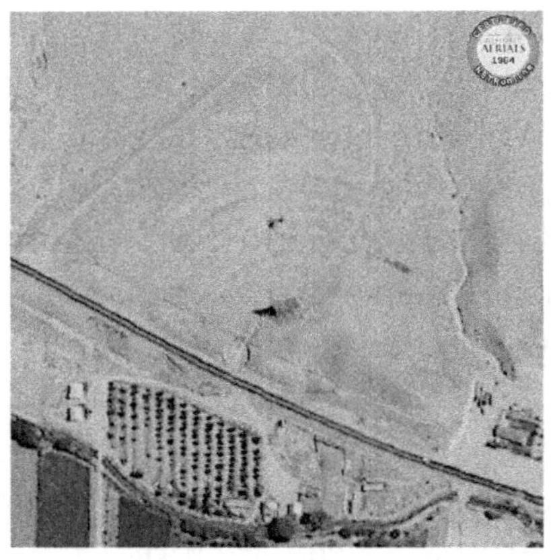

The Mesa Drive-In looked intact in this 1964 photo. Notice Tom Kerby's farm on the south side of the highway. © HistoricAerials.com, used by permission.

running it, the Mesa's final ad in the *Daily Times* was in August 1955. By 1961, the newspaper was referring to the site as the "old Mesa," although the screen stayed intact through at least 1964. A gas well service company occupies the site today.

Valley Drive-In

Location: Less than a mile east of town on then-US 550, now Main Street
Opened: Aug. 11, 1954
Closed: 1985
Capacity: 330 cars

Buoyed by the success of their Apache Drive-In, the Allen theater group started building the area's first widescreen drive-in in the summer of 1954. The site was part of co-owner Kelly Crawford's father-in-law's apple farm. The Valley was the 204th drive-in built by Tom Griffing's experienced construction crew.

An article in *Boxoffice* discussed the changes Russell Allen and Crawford made based on what they learned from the Apache. They built the Valley's concession-projection building with pumice blocks. The glass windows in the snack bar were placed at adult height to prevent children from hanging around inside during the movie. The 35x70-foot screen was made of Flexboard mounted on telephone poles.

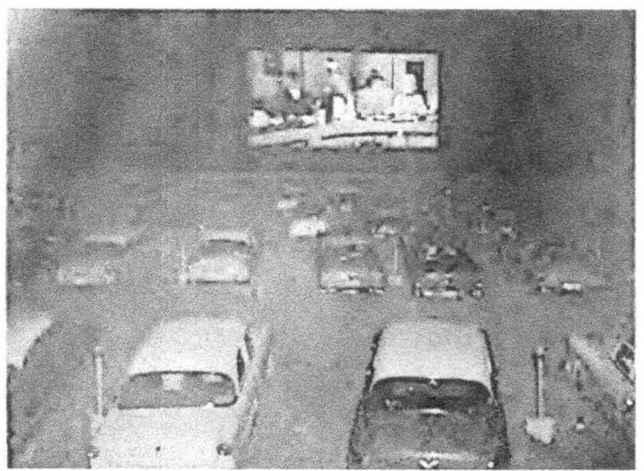

In 1955, *Boxoffice* ran this rare image of the Valley Drive-In during a performance.

The Valley lived a single-owner life, quiet except for the annual Fourth of July fireworks displays. After the 1985 season, Sunwest Bank bought the front of the Valley property to use for a drive-in bank branch. Bank of America now owns the facility, and storage units occupy the Valley's old viewing field.

Intermission: Common Denominators

Some elements of drive-in theaters were so common that they aren't worth mentioning. For example, they all had screens and ticket booths. Similarly, some drive-in stories are so common that I'll just list their categories here.

Young patrons snuck into the drive-in, often in car trunks. In the old days when owners kept most of their ticket money, getting in without paying was taking cash out of drive-in owners' pockets. They hated that. This led to a cat-and-mouse game of carefully judging cars as they came in, and sometimes keeping track of them after they parked.

Dating couples sometimes lost interest in the movie and became more enthusiastic about being with each other. Some of those couples later became parents. I'll leave it at that.

From their beginnings as accidental profit centers to their eventual, modern cafeteria style, concession stands quickly changed to serve more patrons, faster. You can read more about that in a later intermission, Concession Stand Evolution.

Burglars targeted drive-in safes and concession stand cash registers. Robbers loved to hold up box offices. A drive-in would build up a lot of cash on weekends, and it was easy for a motorized bandit to drive up, complete his transaction, and zoom off.

In the mid-1950s, almost all pre-existing drive-ins widened their screens to accommodate CinemaScope and other wide film formats.

In those innocent days of reduced litigation, back when childhood injuries were seen as a rite of passage, drive-ins usually provided playgrounds, mostly in front of the screen. These weren't today's safety-rated plastic fixtures. We're talking 20-foot slides, long seesaws, and puke-inducing spinners, machined out of heavy-duty steel and bolted onto thick, unforgiving slabs of concrete. Parents probably thought it made their kids tougher.

On Sunday mornings, many drive-ins hosted drive-in religious services. This happened a lot every spring on Easter Sunday.

In the 1960s and later, many drive-ins added weekend flea markets.

There are still more obvious common denominators – concentric ramps to tilt the car to the screen, fencing to prevent cars from bypassing the box office, etc. – but let's move forward to the "Indian capital of the world," Gallup.

Gallup

Gallup, the biggest city between Albuquerque and Flagstaff AZ on old Route 66, is home to the El Rancho Hotel. For decades, Hollywood filmmakers used the El Rancho as their base for dozens of productions such as *Billy the Kid* (1930) and *Ace in the Hole* (1951).

Yucca Drive-In

Location: On then-US 66 on the west side of town, just east of the airport
Opened: Sept. 28, 1951
Closed: July 21, 1958
Capacity: 249 cars

William Nagle and Theatre Enterprises, which ran Gallup's indoor theaters, bought a 10-acre site for the city's first drive-in in 1949. Construction was delayed, and the start of the Korean War added restrictions on certain construction materials in theater building. When Nagle finally got a permit from the National Production Authority in the summer of 1951, his project was to be called the Gallup Drive-In. When it opened, it had been renamed the Yucca. Its relatively small screen was supported by five poles 46 feet high.

The Yucca's grand opening went well, but rain

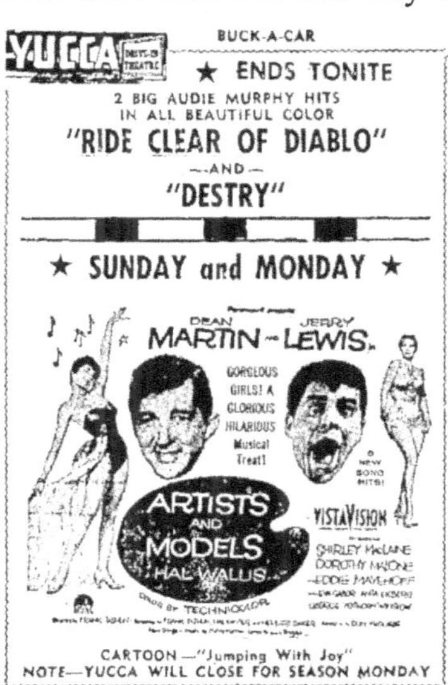

Otherwise typical July 1958 ad for the Yucca, ending with a note that it'll close in the middle of summer.

later that night canceled the following performance. Manager Bruce Waugh said the next day that the drive-in's long access road from US 66 hadn't been surfaced yet, so it would be "too rough for an audience this evening."

By 1957, Nagle was in charge of all of Gallup's movie houses for Frontier Theatres, which turned its attention to the larger, newer Zuni Drive-In on the

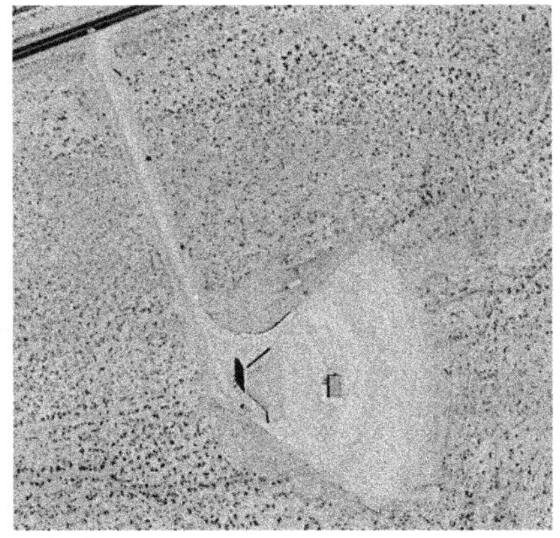

The Yucca was built in the middle of nowhere with a long, straight driveway to Route 66, as seen in this USGS photo from 1952.

other side of town. When the Zuni opened, the Yucca immediately became the second-best drive-in in Gallup, with older films at a cheaper price. That arrangement lasted less than a year. In July 1958, the ad for the Yucca in the *Gallup Daily Independent* abruptly announced a mid-summer season closing date for the drive-in, which never reopened. A grocery store and its parking lot occupy the site today.

Zuni Drive-In

Location: On then-US 66 on the east side of town
Opened: June 4, 1957
Closed: Oct. 3, 1981
Capacity: 578 cars

Longtime Gallup theater man William Nagle oversaw the construction of the Zuni for the Frontier Theaters chain. When it opened, the drive-in sign looked a lot like an old-style Holiday Inn sign, but with the curled arrow cutting between the words instead of going across the top.

Less than three months later, lightning shorted the sound system, but Frontier repaired the system in a day.

In 1968, Commonwealth Theatres bought out Frontier, including the Zuni. The addition of Aztec Avenue between US 66 and the drive-in cut through the drive-in's old driveway entrance, leaving the screen almost adjacent to the new road.

In the 1970s, Zuni manager Bob Sanford attracted patrons with

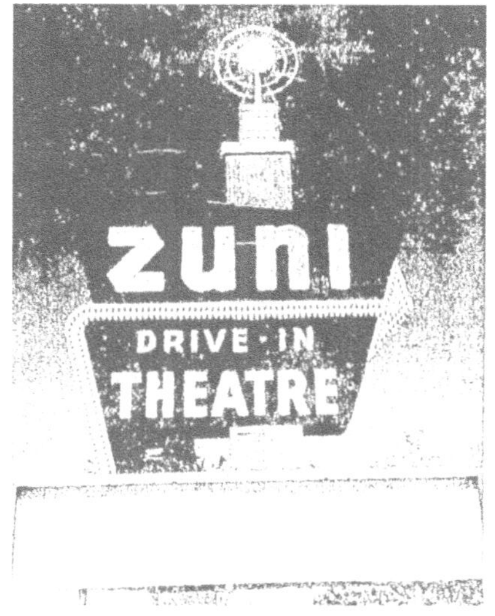

This grainy photo, which probably looked better in 1957 when the *Gallup Independent* published it, is the only image I've found of the Zuni's sign.

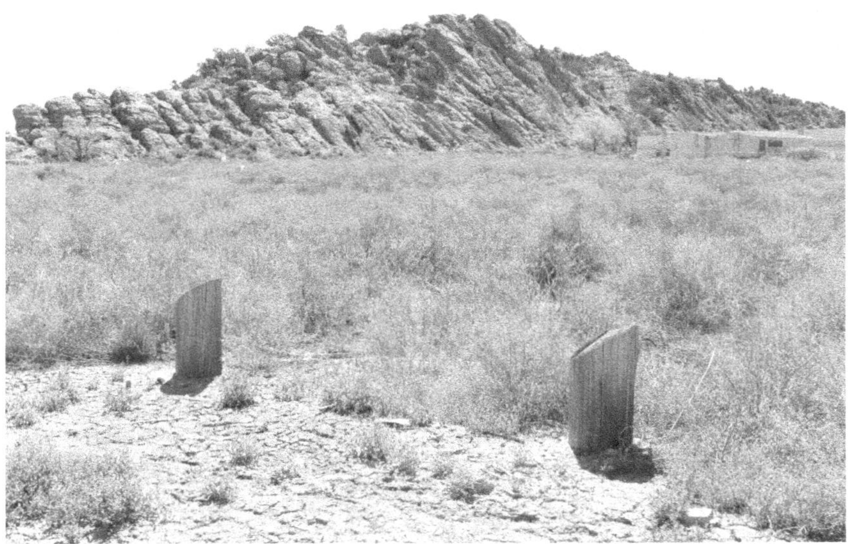

The stumps of the Zuni's wooden screen supports and a brush-covered field of ramps ending in a ragged, rocky ridge continue to furnish a hint of what a night at the movies must have been like. 2019 photo by the author.

promotions such as "Lucky License Night," a watermelon eating contest, and a "Car Smash Night" featuring sledgehammers and a junker automobile.

As the years passed, the Zuni sometimes showed racier films. Its final newspaper ad was for a special program of four R-rated "Fairytale Fantasies." Commonwealth continued to list the Zuni among its holdings in the annual *Motion Picture Almanac* through the 1985 edition, suggesting that it may have been considering re-opening the drive-in. Even that listing ended in 1986.

An elementary school sits where the old concession-projection building had been, but stumps of the old screen tower and overgrown hints of the ramps remain today.

Grants

Three brothers, Angus, John, and Lewis Grant, won the contract to build the Atlantic and Pacific Railroad through here in the 1880s. It became a uranium boom town in the 1950s, and the iconic Uranium Café opened there in 1956.

Also see: Milan.

Sahara Drive-In

Location: On then-US 66 near Redondo Road on the east side of town
Opened: May 1958
Closed: June 1964
Capacity: 300 cars

Jerome "J.C." West's career in the movie business started in Big Spring TX, where he projected films on a white building wall and pumped sound from two large speakers hung from trees. His Terrace Drive-In was a big hit. Looking to expand, West came to Grants in 1950 and bought the indoor Lux Theatre. After building the Trails Drive-In west of town in what would become Milan, he must have liked how well it performed. West's next move was to build the Sahara on the east side of Grants.

The Sahara was a decent-sized drive-in, with room for 300 or 400 cars, depending on the source, and a 58x90-foot screen. After the Sahara was finished, West built his indoor showcase, named the West Theatre, in 1959.

Maybe the small Grants-Milan market could support only one drive-in. For whatever reason, the Sahara operated for barely six years; West shuttered the place in the summer of 1964. After a few years, a trash transfer station moved in and set up shop in the back of the viewing field. Although the West is still an active Route 66 theater, all that's left of the drive-in today is the bottom half of the Sahara sign and marquee at its old entrance.

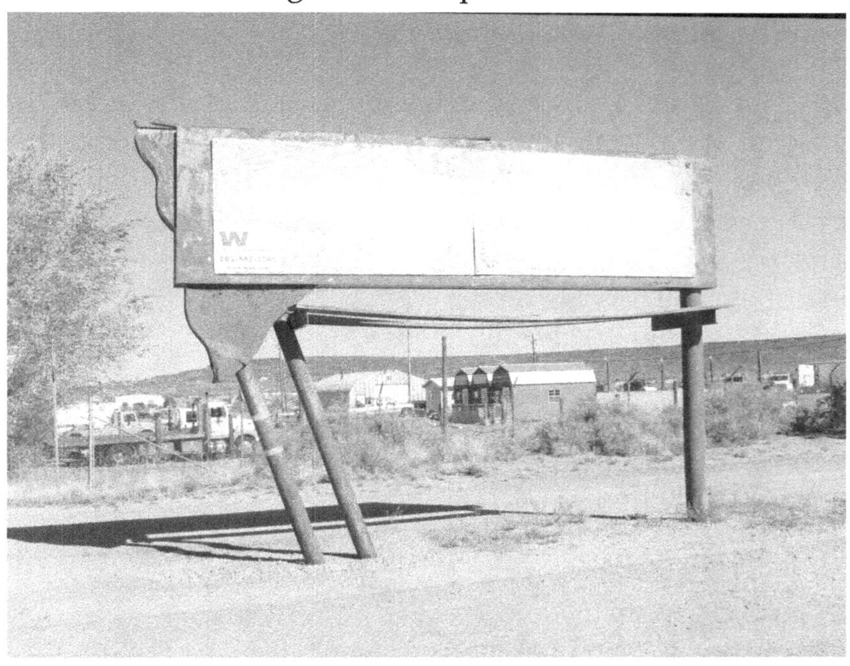

The old Sahara Drive-In sign, at least its bottom half, now directs travelers on old Route 66 to a waste processing facility. 2019 photo by the author.

Hatch

Hatch was originally called Santa Barbara in 1851, and two years later, the US Army built Fort Thorn nearby. The fort closed just a few years later, and the village was re-established in 1875, now named Hatch for Union Army general Edward Hatch. Today, it's known as the Chile Capital of the World, though my main interest is that it was the home of New Mexico's first drive-in.

Drive-In

Location: About a half mile southeast of town on then-US 85, now NM 185
    Opened: Oct. 13, 1946
    Closed: 1948?
    Capacity: 150 cars

This small, unnamed drive-in had a brief life, but it was the first permanent drive-in theater in New Mexico. In October 1946, the *Hatch Reporter* wrote that Dick Allen, owner of the indoor Mission Theatre, was opening a drive-in. It held 150 cars, its screen was 30 feet high, and sound was provided by four large speakers. The following month, *Showmen's Trade Review* reported that "Mrs. S. E. Allen, owner of several New Mexico theatres, has opened a drive-in at Hatch, N. M., which she plans to operate through November before closing for the winter."

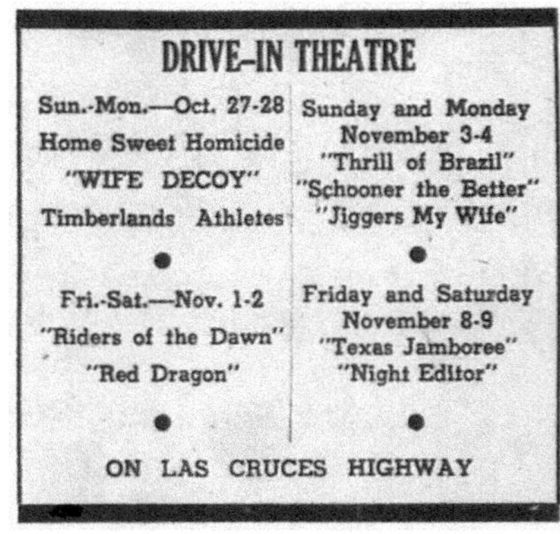

If I could find more back issues of the *Hatch Reporter*, I might learn when the drive-in closed. This ad shows it was still active in November 1948.

At the end of the 1947 season, Mrs. Allen sold the drive-in, along with the indoor Hatch Theatre, to Marlin Butler, who owned two indoor theaters in Albuquerque. Wilson Butler, brought in to manage the Hatch theaters, told *Boxoffice* in February 1948 that the drive-in would be remodeled with in-car speakers and ramps. The drive-in and the Mission, both managed by Dick Allen, bought a joint ad in the back of the Hatch Valley High School 1948 yearbook.

And that's about all I know about Hatch's drive-in. In 1977, Bob Christensen took photos of its triangular adobe screen tower. That was gone by the 1990s; today, two houses occupy the tiny site.

Hobbs

Before I began my research, I would not have guessed that the city with the second-most drive-ins in the state would be Hobbs, which had five. And for a brief period in the mid-1950s, all five were active at the same time. I wish I had access to the newspapers from that period so I could tell you more about them.

Eagle Drive-In

Location: Just west of town on Broadway
Opened: Aug. 8, 1950
Closed: Feb. 9, 1960?
Capacity: 500 cars

In late 1949, E. L. Williamson leased 10 acres from the state of New Mexico and began building Hobbs' second drive-in. He announced that it would be named the Eagle after the local high school sports mascot. For some reason, construction wasn't finished until August the following year. Its screen tower featured a mural of a large eagle, painted by H. R. McBride of Dallas. Lucille Nunnally managed the drive-in, which had a glassed-in concession stand and asphalt-surfaced ramps.

Williamson would soon become an officer in All States Theatres, the company owned by prolific drive-in builder Tom Griffing. It's possible he was already associated with All States when he built the Eagle.

On Feb. 9, 1960, a wind and sandstorm knocked down the Eagle's screen tower. It appears that the drive-in never recovered; I couldn't find any *Hobbs Daily News* ads for it that summer or the summer of 1961. Houses occupy the site of the Eagle's former screen tower, but traces of its back ramps can still be seen today.

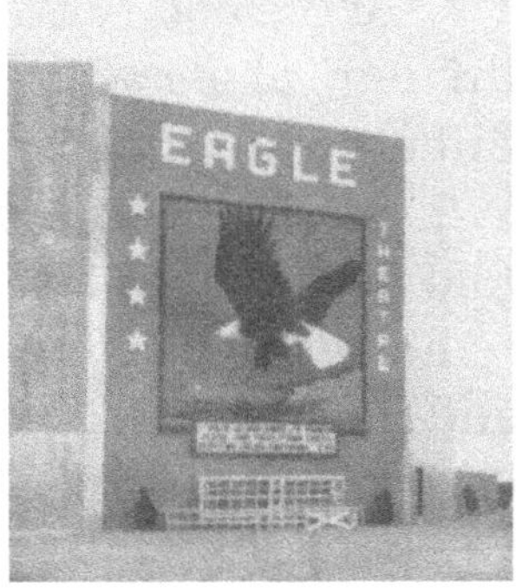

This photo was part of an ad in the 1955 edition of The *Sandstorm*, the Hobbs High School yearbook.

Flamingo Twin Drive-In

Location: Less than a mile north of town on New Mexico 132
Opened: Nov. 24, 1955
Closed: 1984?
Capacity: 1000 cars

The Flamingo Twin was the final drive-in to open in Hobbs but it lasted the longest. All States Theatres built screens facing east and west, opening the drive-in on Thanksgiving Day 1955.

On Feb. 9, 1960, the same sandstorm that knocked out the Eagle Drive-In also twisted at least one of the Flamingo's screens. Unlike the Eagle, the Flamingo reopened.

By 1976, Commonwealth Theatres had taken over the Flamingo Twin. Manager Ricky Littlejohn had a bright red flannel devil outfit, complete with hood, tail, and pitchfork. This was all for a promotion where patrons who could outrun him would win free tickets to see the Peter Fonda movie, "Race with the Devil." *Boxoffice* later reported that the Flamingo didn't have to issue too many passes, since Littlejohn was a former high school track star who could still run well.

In 1982, photographer John Margolies captured a color image of the Flamingo's marquee, showing that it was still active. In the 1984 edition of *Motion Picture Almanac*, Commonwealth still included the Flamingo among its holdings. A 1991 aerial photo showed that the drive-in was long gone. Except for those clues, I'm not sure when Hobbs' last drive-in closed. A strip mall and three residential cul-de-sacs occupy the site today.

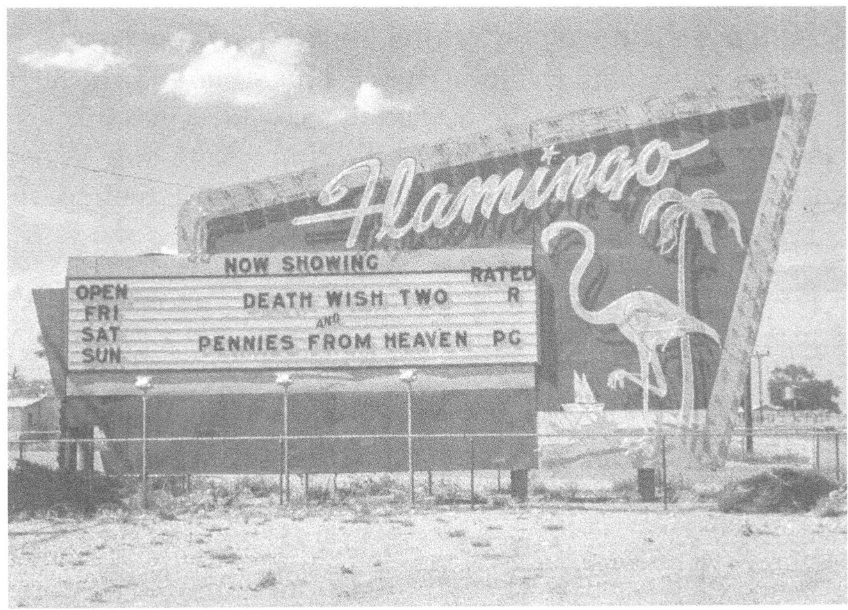

We know that the Flamingo sign was in great shape in 1982 thanks to this photo by John Margolies. It's part of the John Margolies Roadside America photograph archive (1972-2008), Library of Congress, Prints and Photographs Division.

Sky-Vu Drive-In

Location: Just northwest of town on New Mexico 18
Opened: May 5, 1949
Closed: Jan. 28, 1962
Capacity: 350 cars

Theatre Enterprises opened Hobbs' first drive-in in 1949, I believe. A quarter-century later, a retrospective in the *Hobbs Daily News-Sun* suggested that it opened in 1948, but contemporary notes in that newspaper and *Boxoffice* both fixed the "grand opening" date as May 5, 1949.

Manager R. W. Ferguson presided over the new Sky-Vu Drive-In, which included a snack bar in the rear and a playground. For its second season in 1950, Ferguson repainted the screen, repaved the ramps with new blacktop, and added new ramp lights.

At some point, Frontier Theatres bought out Theatre Enterprises, so that's who owned the Sky-Vu when it closed. The last *News-Sun* ad I could find was in mid-winter 1962, an odd time of year to close. A strip mall occupies the site today.

Sunset Drive-In

Location: Northwest of town on Grimes Street, just south of New Mexico 18
Opened: 1954
Closed: April 1957
Capacity: 600 cars

I'm glad that the last two Hobbs drive-ins, alphabetically, line up together. They have a lot in common. They were both built and run by Owen Odell "O. O." Knotts, who lived in a house between them. They both had short lives, and because of gaps in online news coverage, I know very little about either of them. Thank goodness for one stray note indicating that the Trade Wind was the one to the north, or I wouldn't even know which was which.

The Sunset was the second of the pair to open, apparently in 1954. *Motion Picture Almanac* later reported that it held slightly more cars than the Trade Wind. An aerial photo showed a tiny projection booth in the center of the Sunset's viewing field and a larger building, possibly a joint concession stand, in the back between the two drive-ins. In April

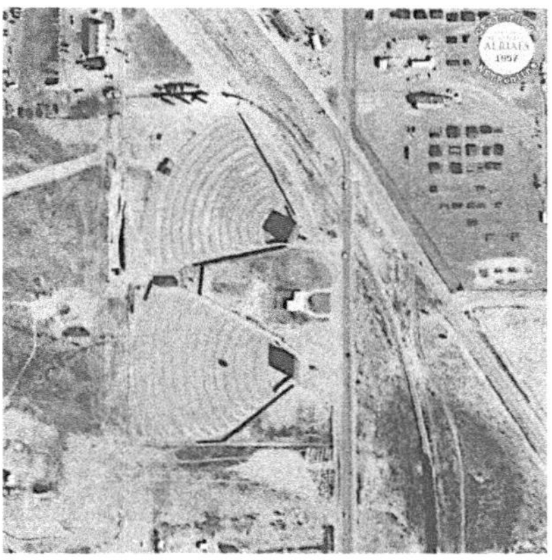

This aerial photo says a lot about the Trade Wind (north) and Sunset. The Trade Wind came first, since it has the larger projection building. The Sunset, with its tiny projection booth, must have shared the concession building near the back rows between the two drive-ins. And there's Mr. Knotts' house between them. © HistoricAerials.com, used by permission.

1957, Knotts sold both of them, plus his house, to Frontier Theatres. The buyers, who owned competing theaters in town, said the Sunset and Trade Wind would be closed "for the time being." They never reopened. Today, a Pizza Inn sits about where the Sunset had been.

Trade Wind Drive-In

Location: Also northwest of town on Grimes Street, just south of New Mexico 18 but north of the Sunset
Opened: 1953?
Closed: April 1957
Capacity: 560 cars

Owen "O. O." Knotts built the Trade Wind, sometimes written as one word, reportedly in 1953. He was already advertising it in the *Hobbs Daily News* by March 3, 1954. For most of the other information about the Trade Wind, check out the listing for the Sunset immediately preceding this one. An oil field equipment supplier occupies the old Trade Wind site today.

Jal

Although Jal is New Mexico's south-easternmost city, its drive-in was neither the farthest south nor farthest east. Anthony's Joy, in the notch next to El Paso TX, was four miles farther south, and the 4-Lane, between Clovis and Texico, was over five miles farther east.

Panther Drive-In

Location: Just south of town on Third Street
Opened: June? 1952
Closed: 1986?
Capacity: 400 cars

Emilu Betty used to own the "Our Drug" store in Jal, and in 1950, she managed the indoor Rex Theatre, owned by Griffith Theatres. Betty left town to manage a drug store in Genoa CO for a year, then returned to the Rex in February 1952. Some time that summer, she opened the Panther Drive-In, although it didn't advertise in the *Jal Record* until January 1953.

What's more confusing is that in 1962, the *Record* wrote that the Panther was built by C. C. Caldwell, who sold it to Bruce Wilkerson and Morris Wood in 1955. Wilkerson later bought out Wood's interest.

By the 1960s Griffith's successor, Frontier Theatres, was running the Panther. Perhaps Frontier always owned the place, employing Betty as a seasoned manager there. In 1968, *Boxoffice* wrote that Norman Pender had taken over the Panther from Wilkerson, who changed jobs to become a policeman. (Wilkerson also owned the Jal's indoor Rex in the 1960s, and Pender owned it in the 1970s, so that purchase was probably a package deal.)

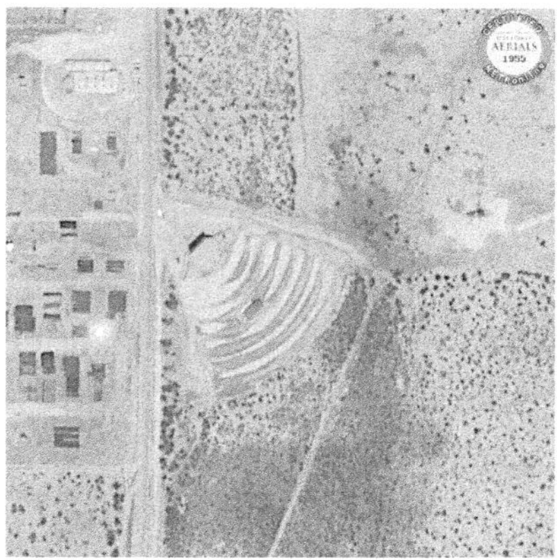

The Panther Drive-In, on the edge of town, had seven concentric ramps. It looks small for its claimed capacity of 400 cars. © HistoricAerials.com, used by permission.

On one evening in April 1969, high winds and possibly a tornado uprooted the Panther's screen and parts of its fence. The concession stand's picture window imploded, knocking out several teeth of one of the workers there. Amazingly, no other reports of car damage or injuries were reported.

In 1977, Larry Stapler bought the Panther "on the spur of the moment" according to a lively article in the *Hobbs News-Sun* seven years later. He built his own AM radio transmitter using television parts and took down the speaker poles. At the time of the 1984 article, Stapler's charcoal-broiled hamburgers were keeping the drive-in in business.

A 1996 aerial photo showed most of the Panther intact, but the screen was gone. Now there are a couple of houses on the old drive-in site. The remains of a small box office building and a few hints of the ramps are the only Panther remnants today.

Las Cruces

Home of New Mexico State University, Las Cruces is the second-most populous city in the state. In its old town area, I recommend La Posta de Mesilla, a restaurant with dazzling atmosphere and flavorful Mexican food in a 180-year-old building.

In his 2015 book, *Screen With a Voice – A History of Moving Pictures in Las Cruces*, David G. Thomas wrote that the Organ Drive-In should be considered the town's third drive-in after the Airdome (opened in 1914 with room for 10 cars and 450 seats) and the Theatre de Guadalupe (1915, 40 cars, 700 seats).

Aggie Drive-In

Location: On US 85 just south of its intersection with US 70/80/180
Opened: May 12, 1966
Closed: 1994
Capacity: 600 cars

Lamar Gwaltney, who ran a few liquor stores, got into the theater business in 1966 by building Las Cruces' third drive-in. His father, Lamar E. Gwaltney, had run an indoor theater in Mena AR for over 15 years before moving to Las Cruces, where he became vice president of the First National Bank. The Aggie's single screen was 90 feet wide by 60 feet high.

It looks like the younger Gwaltney's tenure in the movie business lasted less than a year. Video Independent Theaters bought the Aggie in February 1967, just a month after buying the Fiesta. In 1982, they added a second

The Aggie's ads in the *Las Cruces Sun-News*, even the grand opening, were pretty plain. Can it get plainer than this ad, which ran the day before the Aggie opened?

screen, renaming the drive-in the Aggie Twin, just a couple of months before Allen Theatres bought every movie house in Las Cruces.

The Aggie lasted the longest of all the three local drive-ins, advertising in the New Mexico State student newspaper as late as 1990. Christopher Schurtz wrote in his 2012 book *Historic Las Cruces* that the Aggie closed in 1991, but in February 1995, the *Santa Fe New Mexican* wrote that the Aggie had "closed six months ago". The eastern corner of a large mobile home park occupies the old Aggie site today.

Organ / Fiesta Drive-In

Location: Just southeast of town on Paseo Road
Opened: Aug. 20, 1948
Closed: 1981?
Capacity: 600 cars

Homer Bowington of the El Paso Amusement company built Las Cruces' first drive-in in the summer of 1948. It was called the Organ, named for the nearby Organ Mountains. The *Las Cruces Sun-News* reported that the drive-in's loudspeaker system allowed patrons "to hear just as well with the car windows rolled up as when they are down." Bowington replaced that system with "in-a-car" speakers in 1949.

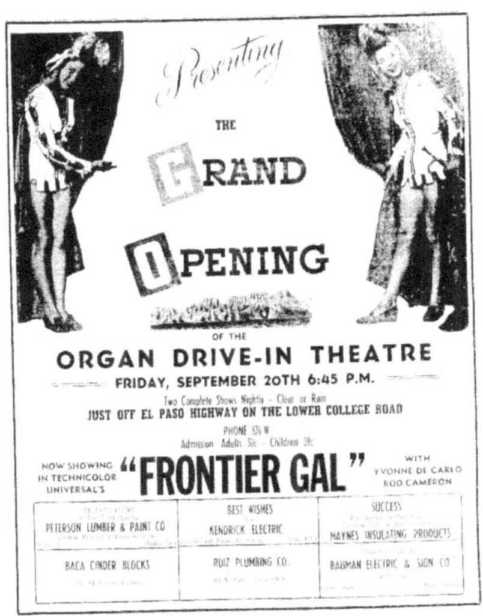

Homer Bowington's company took out a full-page ad to promote the grand opening of the Organ. It included a drawing of the Organ Mountains.

In early 1953, Bowington sold the Organ to Luis Maynes. The drive-in was closed for remodeling on Nov. 3, 1954. When it reopened on Jan. 16, 1955, it had been renamed the Fiesta.

In 1964, the Fiesta added a second screen. Sometime between 1962 and 1965, the Fiesta was sold to El Paso theater man U. A. Kane. I'd bet those two events were related. Flash floods damaged the Fiesta in September 1965, but the drive-in recovered.

Video Independent Theaters bought the Fiesta in January 1967. In 1971, they had to replace the second screen because of new light pollution from nearby businesses. The new screen was metal, closer to the projection booth, and set at a different angle. At the time, manager Ollie Wilhelm said the Fiesta's capacity was 583 cars for the first screen and 458 for the second.

When did the Fiesta close? In February 1981, Wilhelm told the New Mexico State student newspaper that "more people are going to the movies here than ever before." But historian David G. Thomas wrote that the drive-in closed in February 1981, and a 1984 aerial photo showed the Fiesta long gone. An indoor theater, now closed, sits where the Fiesta's original, west screen had been. A strip mall covers the former east viewing field.

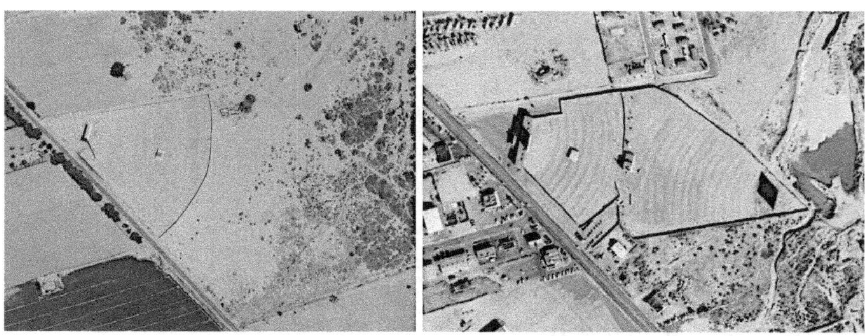

With the original Organ layout (1955) on the left and the twinned Fiesta (1972) on the right, you can see that the owners carved off a back row from the first viewing field and shifted the entrance to the back. © HistoricAerials.com, used by permission.

Rocket Drive-In

Location: Just north of town on US 70
Opened: July 20, 1952
Closed: Nov. 14, 1965
Capacity: 500 cars

U. A. Kane must have been a character. Sometimes referred to as Hugh or Al, he had a hand in many of the theaters in El Paso and Las Cruces. In particular, Kane built the Rocket in Las Cruces.

The drive-in soon added a miniature train in 1953, proclaiming, "This is a miniature of the General Motors Diesel Electric, with air brakes and all. It is the only one of its kind in the Southwest or Rocky Mountain District." But it wasn't there for long; Kane's ad in the Oct. 23, 1954 issue of *Boxoffice* offered to sell it with 750 feet of "like new" rail.

The Rocket upgraded its screen in 1957 and continued operating for just a few more years. Not long after Kane had acquired the Fiesta and (probably) added a second screen, he seemed to lose interest in Rocket. He dismantled it in early 1966, and I'll bet that Kane reused parts of it when he built the Rocket Drive-In in El Paso later that year. A cluster of commercial buildings occupies the Las Cruces Rocket's former site.

ROCKET DRIVE-IN

We are open every night at 7.

Don't miss our beautiful Snack Bar!

Main Street on Hi-way 70

Our Projection Room is completely equipped with RCA sound equipment and operated by International Alliance of Theatrical Stage Employees and Moving Picture Machine Operators of the United States and Canada.

LAS CRUCES LOCAL. NO. 843

The management of the Rocket used to get chatty in their newspaper ads, such as this one from opening night in 1952.

Las Vegas

"The original" Las Vegas, established in 1835, is most notable in this book for having the state's last operating drive-in theater that was built in the 20th Century. It's also home to the only surviving Carnegie Library in New Mexico and the recently restored Castañeda Hotel, a former Harvey House by the train station.

Vegas Drive-In

Locations: First, about 1½ miles north of town on US 85; second, on the south side of town on US 85
Opened: March? 1950
Closed: Oct. 10, 1958 or Oct. 14, 1960
Capacity: 350 cars

Las Vegas man Gus Daskalos and Green River WY's Steve Nitse built Las Vegas's first drive-in, opening it to capacity crowds. But when, exactly? The first local ad I could find was March 6, 1950. The Vegas used red, yellow, and blue lights on a 60-foot pole in the back of the viewing field to simulate soft moonlight. By the end of its first season, it had a children's playground in front of the screen.

That's most of what I know about the Vegas. As many drive-ins did in the 1950s, the Vegas filed a federal anti-monopoly lawsuit because it couldn't get first-run movies. The story was reported in the

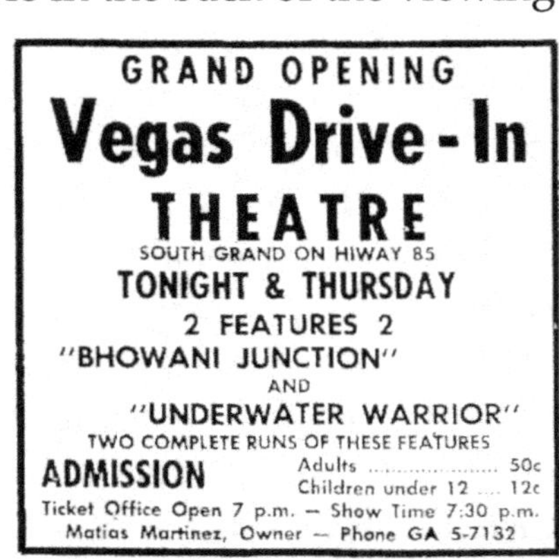

The second, short-lived version of the Vegas had its grand opening in June 1960.

Denver Post on Nov. 23, 1958, when the drive-in was still owned by Daskalos and Nitse. I never saw any results from the lawsuit, but I can't recall any similar suit ever succeeding. In early 1959, all of the drive-in's equipment, speakers, buildings, and signage were sold, and the Vegas never reopened.

Or did it? On June 8, 1960, an advertisement appeared in the *Las Vegas Daily Optic* for the Vegas Drive-In, "south on Highway 85," owned by Matias Martinez, the name of a local grocery owner. Did Martinez buy the old Vegas Drive-In stuff and move it to the other side of town? The new drive-in's final advertisement in the *Daily Optic* appeared on October 14 that year.

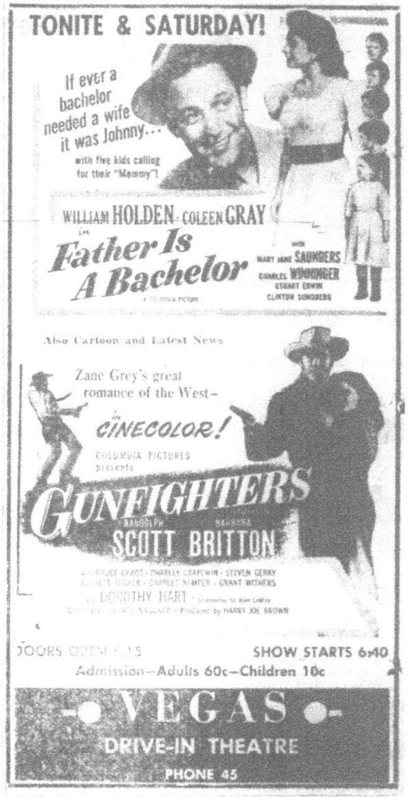

This is the first ad I could find for the Vegas Drive-In, from March 1950. It doesn't look much like a grand opening.

In April 1961, the second Vegas Drive-In made regional news after winds knocked down its screen. Arthur Martinez, son of the owner, estimated the loss at $8,000. There's no evidence that the drive-in ever reopened, and there's no direct evidence that it was related to the first Vegas.

An aerial photo taken in August 1960 placed the second Vegas at 300 S. Grand Avenue, with a size close to that of the first Vegas Drive-In. It was completely gone by a 1981 photo, and nothing remains of it today.

Fort Union Drive-In

Location: Just north of town at 3300 7th Street
Opened: May? 1960
~~**Closed:**~~ open!
Capacity: 350 cars

The Fort Union Drive-In opened in 1960 sometime between April 24, when its snack bar was shown under construction, and May 22, when its first ad appeared in the *Las Vegas Daily Optic*'s Sunday edition. The following January, *Boxoffice* published a list of new drive-ins, noting that the Fort Union was owned by John Wolfe. That was the only time I've seen that name with the Fort Union. By its belated first appearance in the *Motion Picture Almanac*'s annual drive-in list, the Fort Union was owned by Les Dollison.

Dollison happened to visit town in April 1968 to update the drive-in's sound and projection equipment and to revamp the "Bugle Call" concession stand. That was when he appointed John "Johnny" Aragon, Jr. as manager, a position he would hold for the rest of the Fort Union's first life.

In February 1976, Aragon took out a newspaper ad to say simply that the Fort Union was not for sale. What did happen in June that year was Aragon's promotion to regional supervisor of the Dollison theaters, leaving brother-in-law Gene Lujan in charge whenever Aragon's duties took him out of town.

The Fort Union closed for three years in the 1980s. It was also filmed as a Russian concentration camp for the 1984 movie Red Dawn. Meanwhile, Gilbert Pino built a ranch house 100 yards from the screen. Looking over at the closed drive-in, Pino "didn't want somebody to take it over and turn it into something I didn't like," he later told

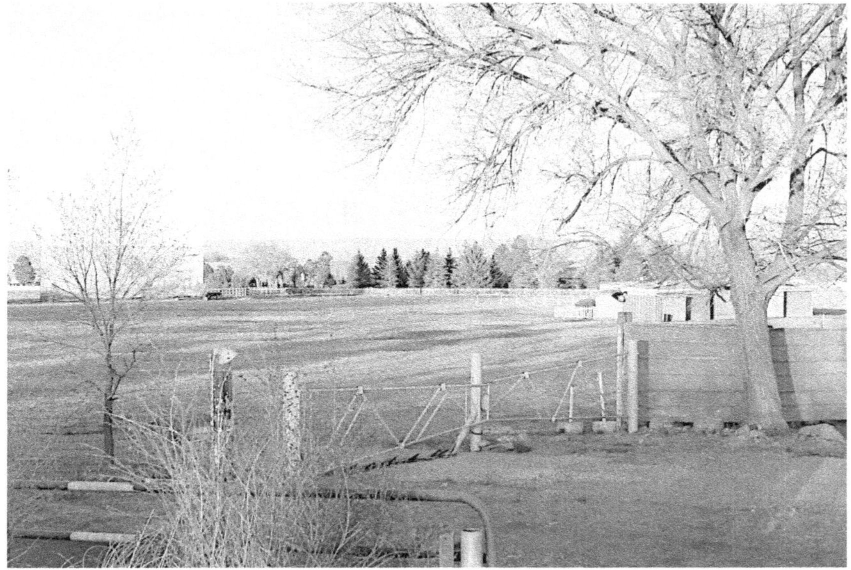

The last active drive-in in New Mexico still looks good these days. 2013 photo by the author.

the *Albuquerque Journal*. Pino bought the Fort Union for $45,000 and reopened it in 1989.

For the rejuvenated drive-in, Pino hired former local indoor theater manager Jeanna DiLucchio, who added FM radio sound. She also reached out to Aragon, who had moved on to restaurants, for the recipe to a Fort Union customer favorite, the drive-in's green chili-topped pizza.

The Fort Union's next crisis hit after the 2013 season, when movie studios switched from film to digital projection. DiLucchio and city business owners tried to raise the money for an expensive new projector, but fell short. Jake Cordova, then a teenager who had worked at the drive-in, asked his grandfather, former Taos County sheriff Felipe Cordova, to buy the projector and take over the Fort Union. The elder Cordova agreed. For the 2014 season, Jake became general manager of the last drive-in in New Mexico, with DiLucchio still helping to book movies for the place. Knock on wood, it's still active today.

Lordsburg

The eastbound I-10 New Mexico Welcome Center is in Lordsburg. The city is near the start of the Continental Divide Trail, and is the trail's lowest point at just under 4200 feet. Lordsburg resident Elizabeth Garrett, daughter of famed sheriff Pat Garrett, wrote the official New Mexico state song, "O Fair New Mexico."

Chief Drive-In

Location: About three miles east of town on then-US 70/80
Opened: April 17, 1954
Closed: Aug. 30, 1964
Capacity: 250 cars

The woman who earlier opened New Mexico's first drive-in in Hatch, Mrs. S. E. Allen, built a drive-in in her home town of Lordsburg in the spring of 1954. When the Chief opened, the *Lordsburg Liberal* wrote that it had "speakers for 225 cars." The *Motion Picture Almanac* listed it with room for 250. Allen apparently ran the Chief for all of its 11 seasons.

The last Chief ad I could find in the *Liberal* was Aug. 28, 1964. After showing movies through Aug. 30, the ad ended with, "Drive-in closes after Sunday show for

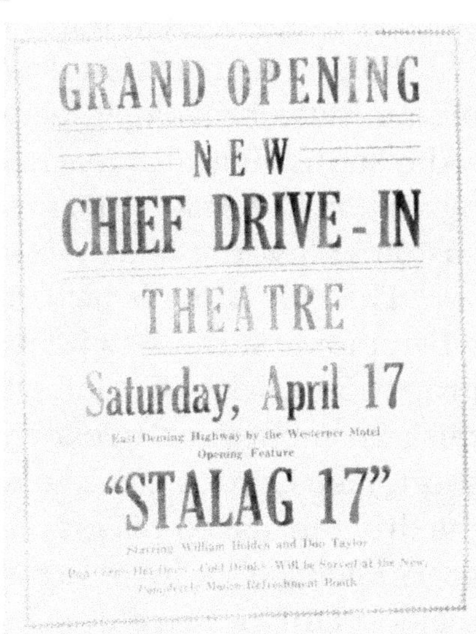

The Chief's grand opening ad emphasized the treats available at the snack bar.

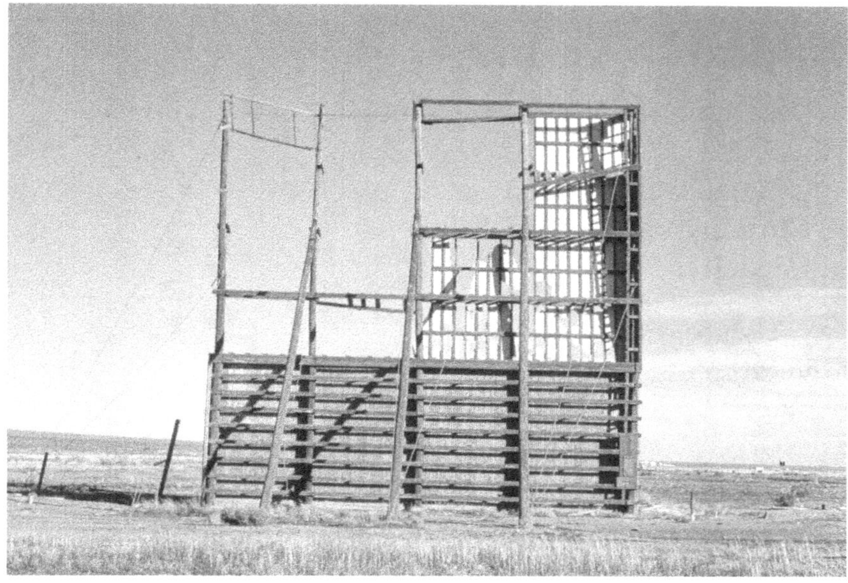

The old Chief Drive-In screen must have disintegrated in place for years. This is how it looked in 1979. From the John Margolies Roadside America photo archive of the Library of Congress.

winter months." Spot checks of summer 1965 issues showed ads for the indoor Coronado but nothing for the Chief.

In 1979, John Margolies photographed the very tattered remains of the Chief's screen, an image now available from the Library of Congress. The site remains an empty lot today, with faint reminders of the ramps still visible.

Lovington

Jim and Robert Love founded this city in 1908. Robert wanted to call it Loving, but the USPS rejected that name because there was already a Loving NM southeast of Carlsbad. Lovington's population took off after the Denton pool of underground oil was discovered in 1950.

Wildcat Drive-In

Location: About 1½ miles southeast of town on New Mexico 18
Opened: Sept. 9. 1953
Closed: Aug. 31, 1975
Capacity: 500 cars

Theatre Enterprises opened Lovington's second drive-in in 1953, managed by Jodie Wiest. A cyclone extensively damaged the Wildcat in April 1954, just a few months after it opened. The drive-in also survived a man-made mishap in September 1964, when a car plowed through part of a building, causing $4,000 in damages.

(Historian note: There was also a Wildcat Drive-In *restaurant* in Lovington around this time.)

Frontier Theatres took over for Theatre Enterprises in the early 1960s, and Commonwealth Theatres bought Frontier's drive-ins in 1968. The Wildcat's final ad in the *Lovington Daily Leader* showed a schedule of movies through the Sunday before Labor Day 1975. Although Commonwealth continued to include the Wildcat among its holdings in the annual *Motion Picture Almanac* circuit list through 1984, a 1983 aerial photo showed that the drive-in's screen was gone. A cluster of industrial buildings occupies the site today.

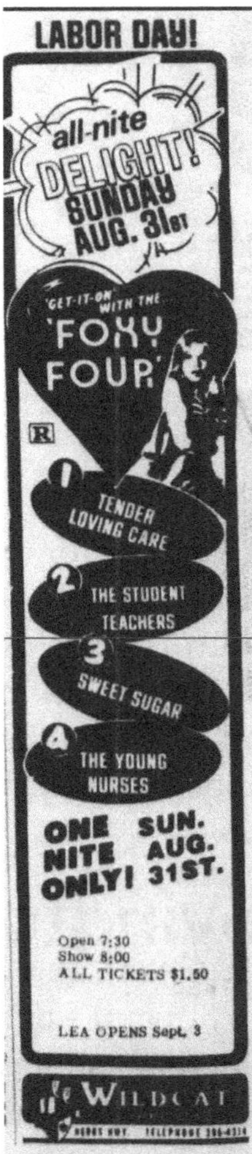

The Wildcat's final ad in the *Lovington Daily Leader*.

Yucca Drive-In

Location: Less than a half mile west of town on US 82
Opened: Sept. 21, 1951
Closed: 1957?
Capacity: 201 cars

Griffith Theatres announced in the summer of 1948 that construction was underway on a 600-car drive-in in Lovington, with a projected opening before the end of the year. I don't know whatever came of that. Over two years later, Theatre Enterprises said in December 1950 that its drive-in would open early in 1951. It turned out that the opener was delayed until September, but the Yucca finally opened, managed by Alvah Haley.

The *Lovington Leader*'s theater ads were spotty at best in the mid-1950s, making it difficult to tell when the Yucca closed. In 1958, the *Leader* ran ads for the indoor Lea and the Wildcat, but not the Yucca. The *Motion Picture Almanac*, notoriously slow in noticing closures, dropped the Yucca from its annual drive-in list in 1961. A 1964 topographical map showed Taylor Junior High School where the Yucca had been. A block of houses occupies the site today.

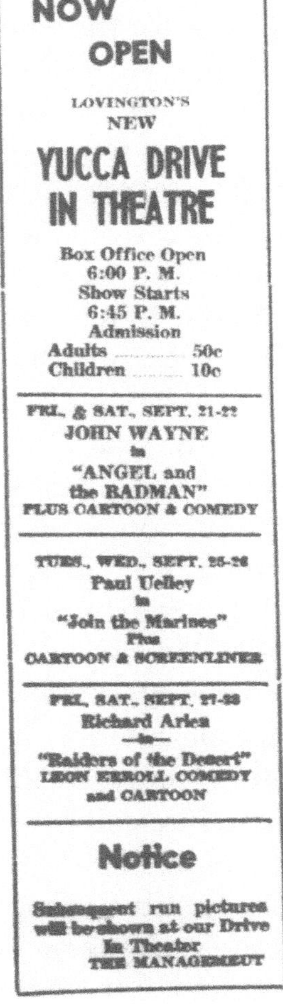

The Yucca's first ad in the *Lovington Daily Leader* wasn't quite a grand opening.

Intermission:
Films Made in New Mexico

There have been films made in New Mexico since before it was a state. In 1897, Thomas Edison shot about a minute of children walking at the Isleta Day School. Between 1910 and 1917, Tom Mix shot more than 100 short movies for the Selig Polyscope Company in Las Vegas. But with the advent of sound, more westerns were shot closer to the studios' home in California.

Hollywood began to rediscover New Mexico in the 1940s and 50s. In *Ace in the Hole* (1951), the cliffs near Gallup are practically the main character. The residents of Grant County were featured in *Salt of the Earth* (1954), based on a real-life miners' strike a few years earlier. However, film productions in the state were occasional at best.

The spark that ignited New Mexico's modern film production industry came from David Cargo, governor of the state from 1967 to 1970. He visited Hollywood to promote New Mexico as a film destination, and more importantly, established the state film commission, now the New Mexico Film Office. The number of movies made in the state grew from about a dozen in the decade before Cargo became governor to about 100 in the decade after he left office.

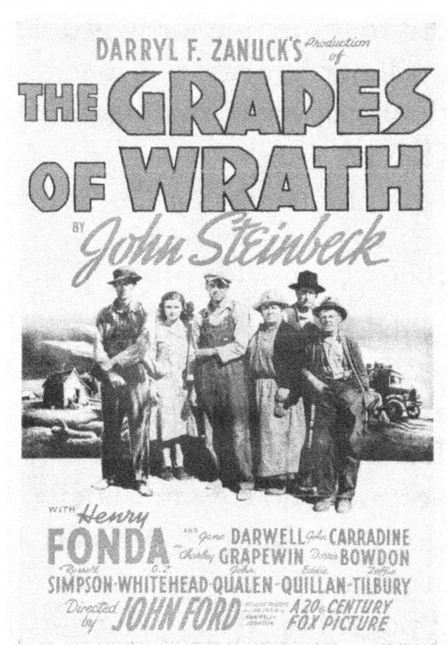

Parts of *The Grapes of Wrath* (1940) were shot in Gallup, Laguna Pueblo, and Santa Rosa.

Today, the Film Office coordinates financial incentives offered by the state government to film studios doing work in New Mexico. For example, Netflix purchased a studio in Albuquerque in 2018 and has since expanded it. NBC Universal opened a projection studio in a former Albuquerque warehouse in 2021. The state's wide-open spaces, experienced film support personnel, and generous cash supplements should keep the movie industry going strong there for years to come.

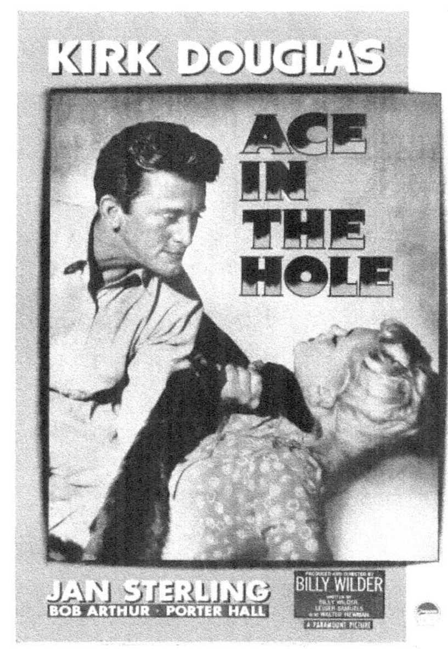

If you've ever seen *Ace in the Hold* (1951), you're reminded of it every time you drive west of Gallup.

From the comprehensive list provided by the NMFO, I've compiled the Top 20 movies filmed (at least in part) in New Mexico. The rankings are based on the average rating of IMDb users, with a minimum of 2000 votes as of February 2023.

Jurassic Park (released 1993) 8.2 rating / 999k votes
No Country for Old Men (2007) 8.2 / 986k
Indiana Jones and the Last Crusade (1989) 8.2 / 762k
Logan (2017) 8.1 / 774k
The Grapes of Wrath (1940) 8.1 / 95k
Ace in the Hole (1951) 8.1 / 37k
The Avengers (2012) 8.0 / 1.4M
The Big Country (1958) 7.9 / 19k
The House I Live In (2012) 7.9 / 5.3k
Captain Fantastic (2016) 7.8 / 222k

Brokeback Mountain (2005) 7.7 / 363k
3:10 to Yuma (2007) 7.7 / 317k
Sorcerer (1977) 7.7 / 23k
True Grit (2010) 7.6 / 344k
21 Grams (2003) 7.6 / 240k
Hell or High Water (2016) 7.6 / 236k
Traffic (2000) 7.6 / 210k
The Muppet Movie (1979) 7.6 / 37k
Lonely Are the Brave (1962) 7.6 / 9.3k
Beyond the Blackboard (2011) 7.6 / 2.3k

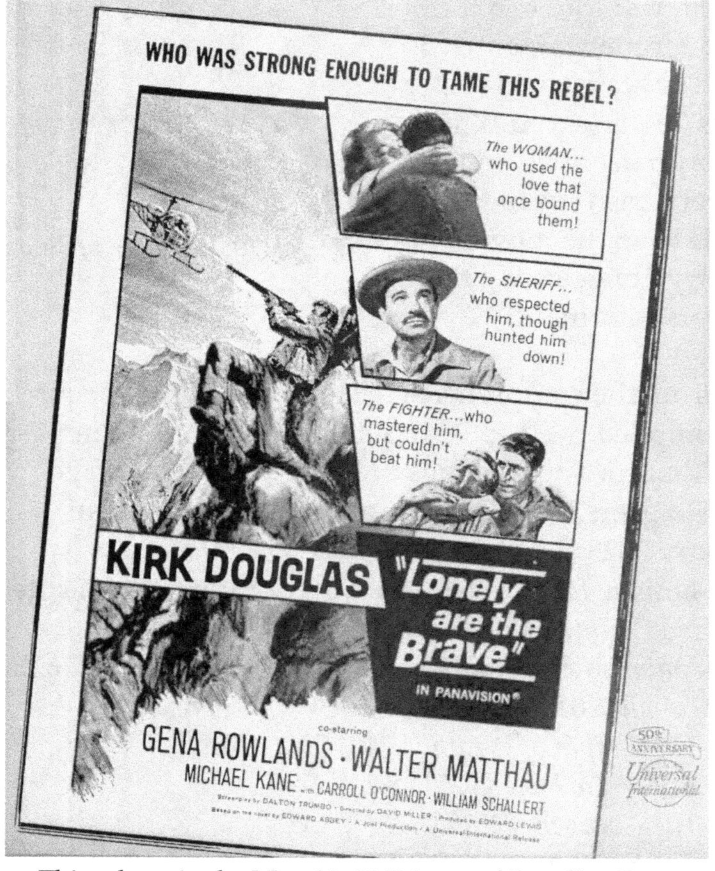

This ad ran in the May 14, 1962 issue of *Boxoffice*. Two
months later, the magazine reported that New
Mexico's largest city had branded itself AlbuKIRKee
in honor of the local premiere of *Lonely Are the Brave*.

Milan

In 1957, landowner Salvador Milan wanted to be annexed by Grants, but the city was unable to buy the water company that served his property. Instead, the village of Milan formed that year. The Motel Milan, a Route 66 icon, was built in 1946 and restored as a trading post decades later.

Trails Drive-In

Location: In the middle of town, two blocks west of US 66 at East Street
Opened: March? 1954
Closed: 1984?
Capacity: 225 cars

J. C. West came to Grants from Big Spring TX in 1950, and his first construction project was the Trails, then two miles outside of town in an unincorporated area. In April 1953, he told Boxoffice that he had bought $15,000 worth of equipment for his drive-in. In early September, *Boxoffice* wrote that the Trails would open later than month, but in January 1954, the magazine said it would open "early in the spring." The 1954 opener could have been a season opener, but my guess is that delays pushed the Trails past its original target to the following season.

The Trails was small, about one small city block, although it was in the middle of nowhere when it was built. It had a wide screen facing

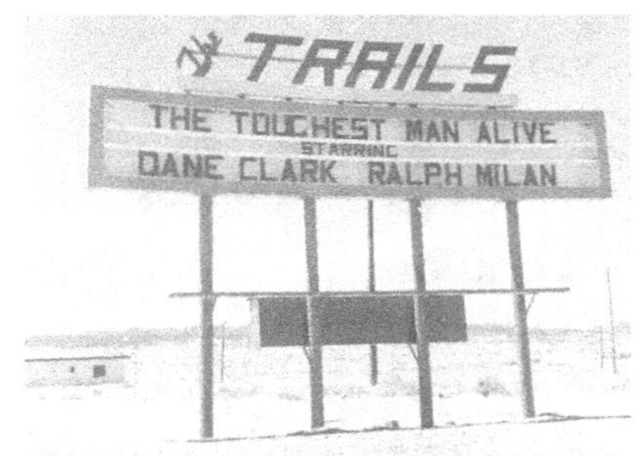

"Nlister" posted this undated photo of the Trails' sign at CinemaTreasures.org.

northeast. Patrons would pay at the single box office at the back of the viewing field.

It sounds like West grew tired of running the Grants-Milan theaters. He opened an indoor theater in Albuquerque, and in 1975, he and a partner opened a recording studio there. West started another career in music, as a promoter, manager, and sound engineer for bands. In January 1977, Theatre Operators, based in Bozeman MT, leased the Grants-Milan theaters and eventually bought them.

The Trails was still operating in 1983, when the *Albuquerque Journal* mentioned it in passing. In September 1984, Theater Operators sold the drive-in to former city manager Roy McDowell. I'm not certain that the Trails was still active then, and I don't know whether McDowell ever reopened it. Hints of the old ramps and concession stand foundation are still there today.

Portales

Portales was named after a nearby watering hole near a rocky ledge resembling a Spanish porch. Its first mayor, Washington Ellsworth Lindsey, later became governor of New Mexico. The area is the top producer of certified organic peanut butter in the country, thanks to its abundance of Valencia peanuts.

Crawley's Drive-In

Location: Just over a mile northeast of town on US 70
Opened: 1953?
Closed: 1956?
Capacity: 200 cars

Perry Crawley was born in Texas in 1918, and by 1954 he was a member of the Texico school board. In 1956, probably after closing his short-lived drive-in, Crawley moved to Phoenix to open a Baird's Bakery. Except for his 65-year marriage to his wife, that's about all I know about the man who built Portales' second, short-lived drive-in.

I know even less about Crawley's Drive-In. It looked intact in a 1954 aerial photo, and Crawley's appeared in both the 1956 *Motion Picture Almanac*

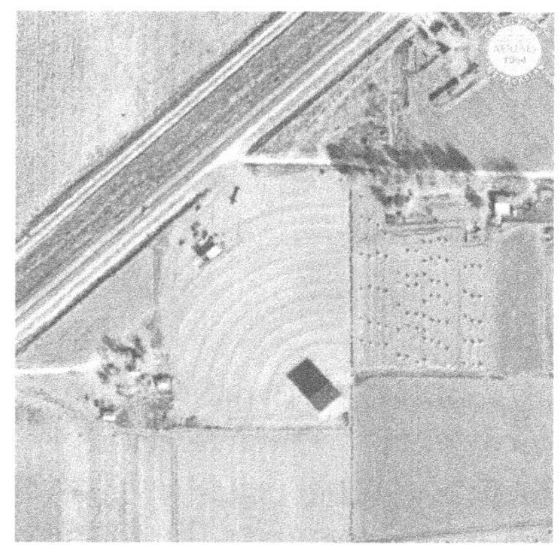

This 1954 aerial photo is the most concrete evidence of Crawley's Drive-In's existence. © HistoricAerials.com, used by permission.

drive-in list and the 1955-56 *Theatre Catalog*. It was gone by the time the 1957 *MPA* was published. A 1979 aerial photo showed no trace of the former Crawley's. It's still a flattened, vacant lot today.

Varsity Drive-In

Location: Less than a mile southwest of town on US 70
Opened: April 9, 1950
Closed: 1981?
Capacity: 250 cars

Theatre Enterprises opened the Portales' first drive-in, the Varsity, on Easter Sunday on what was then known as the Elida highway. Russel Ackley managed the Varsity when it opened; by the end of the season, the manager was Cliff Kelm.

A columnist for the *Portales News Tribune* later remembered that Sunday nights were Spanish-language movie nights. Helena Rodrigues wrote, "Before we went, I remember Dad popping a big brown paper bag full of popcorn on the stove, back when you could take your own food."

The Varsity lived a full corporate-owned life. By the early 1960s, Frontier Theatres had taken over for Theatre Enterprises, and Commonwealth Theatres bought Frontier's drive-ins in 1968. In March 1978, the indoor Tower Theatre burned down, so the movies that had been booked to show there moved to the Varsity.

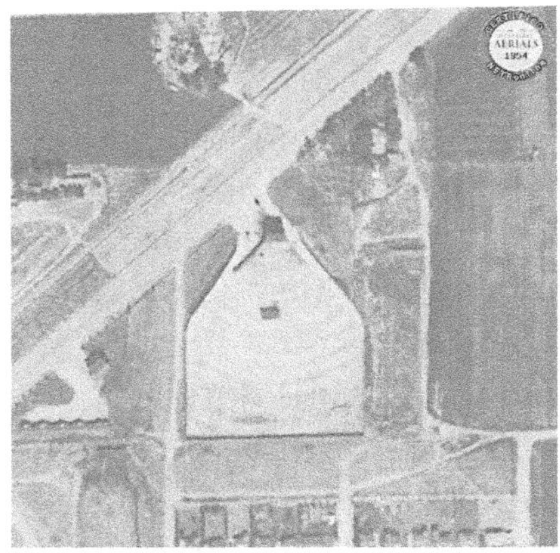

The Varsity Drive-In looked like it was built with a standardized layout. 1954 photo © HistoricAerials.com, used by permission.

The last note I could find for movies at the Varsity was in August 1981. It was still intact in a 1983 aerial photo. In 1996, the *Albuquerque Journal* wrote that a Super 8 motel had taken its place. It's still there today.

Raton

Raton sits just a few miles south of Raton Pass, a critical part of the Santa Fe Trail's mountain branch, the Atchison, Topeka & Santa Fe Railway, and now I-25. It was the site of New Mexico's first horse racetrack, La Mesa Park, which closed in 1992, and of the Shuler Theater, opened in 1915 and still operating today.

85 Drive-In

Location: A mile south of the railroad tracks on US 64/85

Opened: June 15, 1949

Closed: 2004

Capacity: 350 cars

In early 1949, Floyd Davis of Springfield CO and Nat Jones of Abernathy TX built the 85 Drive-In, named for its highway. In October of that year, a fully loaded school bus took full advantage of the drive-in's $1 per car night. One month later, at the end of a successful season, Davis and Jones sold the 85 to J. E. Oliver, owner of the local Plaza Food store.

Oliver kept the 85 for one season, selling it in September 1950 to regional theater owners Hubbard & Murphy. By the early 1960s, Bernard J. McKenna was operating the 85 along with Raton's indoor El Raton Theatre. In the 1977 *Motion Picture Almanac*, Murphy was listed again as the 85's owner.

In the 1990s, I was running a Colorado drive-in theater website. I kept an ear out for news of the 85, since it's so close to the border. My memory is that it was closed for some seasons during its late run, but I don't have any hard evidence of that. In a New Mexico drive-in roundup article from the Associated Press, published in the *Alamogordo Daily News* on May 10, 1998, the owner of Carlsbad's Fiesta said, "To my knowledge, the 85 Drive-In in Raton will open this year."

The *Albuquerque Journal* included it as one of four active New Mexico drive-ins in a May 7, 2000 article. The 85 was described as still using in-car speakers, and had a "historic, pueblo-style snack bar and projection booth."

On Oct. 1, 2004, the *Albuquerque Tribune* gave us a near-perfect time capsule of what would be the 85's final weeks. It was run by Loren Eigenberg, then 69 years old, the ex-husband of owner Frances Murphy.

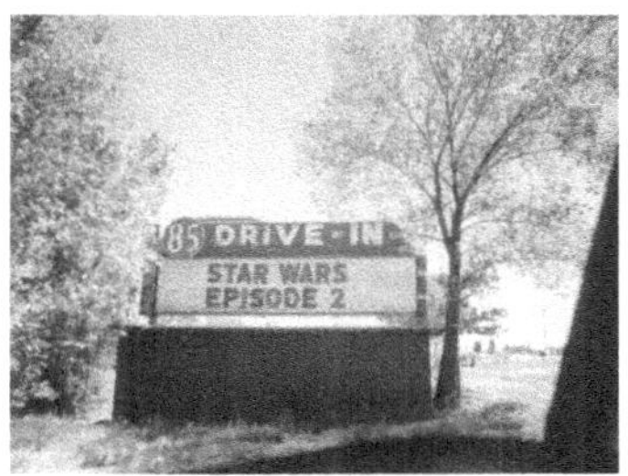

The 85's sign as it looked in 2002. Photo by "dallasmovietheaters," posted at Cinema-Treasures.org.

Eigenberg said he had run the 85 for 33 years, "And this might be the last." The drive-in switched to FM sound for its final season.

Although the *Tribune* article said that a commercial developer had a deposit on the property, the old 85 site remains vacant today. Its screen, still intact in a 2005 aerial photo, was gone by 2009, though hints of the ramps and the concession stand foundation are still there.

Regina

Regina is a small census-designated place on NM 96 in Sandoval County. It's small, home to about 100 people. In his book *The Place Names of New Mexico*, Robert Hixson Julyan wrote that it was named after the capital of Saskatchewan. Regina is home to Regina Mercantile, where you can buy gasoline, bagged ice, groceries, and much more.

Frontier Drive-In

Location: On New Mexico 96 a quarter mile south of its intersection with then-NM 95

Opened: 1959?
Closed: 1968?
Capacity: 100 cars

This tiny drive-in in a tiny settlement is another that I know almost nothing about. A 1963 aerial photo showed it with a south-southeast-facing screen and three or four small ramps. The Frontier Drive-In was listed in the 1966 *Motion*

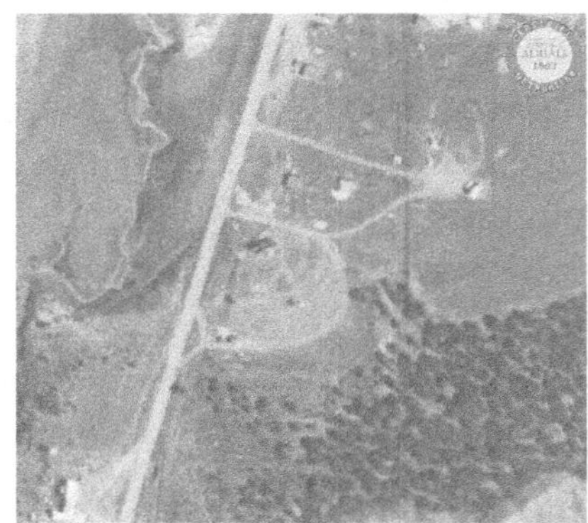

You can barely see the tiny Frontier Drive-In. 1963 photo © HistoricAerials.com, used by permission.

Picture Almanac with a capacity 100 cars, owned by H. C. Lancaster. The *Film Daily Year Book* listed even less, just its name and town, in its 1964-1968 editions.

The only other mention I've found was part of the *Albuquerque Journal*'s Aug. 11, 1996 roundup of state drive-in histories. "Tiny (population 80) and remote (far up on the Continental Divide), Regina regularly drew a crowd to its Frontier Drive-In, now deceased." If you hear anything about the place, please let me know.

Roswell

Roswell might have been just another regional hub with a nearby military base. But that base, then called Roswell Army Air Field, was the eventual destination of the weather balloon debris found on Mac Brazel's ranch in 1947. "The Roswell Incident" became a conspiracy theorists' favorite, and today the city is home to the International UFO Museum.

Ballojak Drive-In

Location: A half mile south of town on Main Street, the road to Walker Air Force Base
Opened: July 27, 1951
Closed: Sept. 20, 1970
Capacity: 500 cars

Theatre Enterprises must have liked how well their Starlite Drive-In was performing in Roswell, because it quickly began construction on two more. The company announced one new project in October 1950, and my guess is it's the drive-in that became the Ballojak, although the Jingle Bob opened days later.

By the way, I've seen this drive-in spelled many different ways. The 1952 *Theatre Catalog* listed it as the

Ballo Jak, the *Motion Picture Almanac* called it the Ballo-Jack, and in 2020, a *Roswell Daily Record* article remembered it as the Ball-O-Jak. However, most of its early-1960s ads in the *Daily Record* were for the single, eight-letter word Ballojak (with an occasional Ballojack thrown in), so that's how I'm spelling it here.

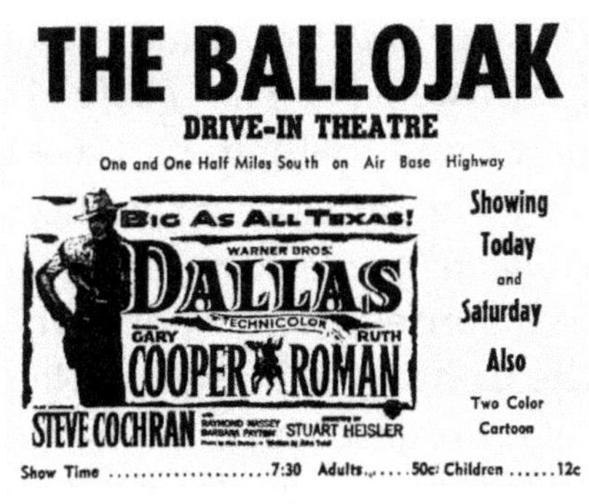

The Ballojak's first ad in the *Roswell Daily Record*.

In February 1953, Theatre Enterprises offered patrons a free gallon of gas (to run their car heaters) when the temperature dropped below 50 degrees.

As with several other New Mexico drive-ins, ownership passed to Frontier Theatres, then to Commonwealth Theatres. After running ads during the 1970 season, the Ballojak had stopped advertising by September 22 that year. A bottling plant occupies the site today, though remnants of the last few ramps are still visible behind it.

Cactus Drive-In

Location: On Poe Street a half mile east of the fairgrounds
Opened: 1963?
Closed: 1975?
Capacity: 300 cars

The Cactus Drive-In opened between 1961, when an aerial photo showed the remains of an old race track at its future site, and August 1964, when it was mentioned in a story in the *Roswell Daily Record*. The Cactus showed mostly, perhaps exclusively, Spanish-language films, which may be why it didn't advertise much in the *Daily Record*.

On September 22, 1970, just after the closing of the Ballojak left Roswell with only one other drive-in, the Cactus ran an advertisement noting that it was "Now Open" with some English-language features. I don't think that change of direction lasted long.

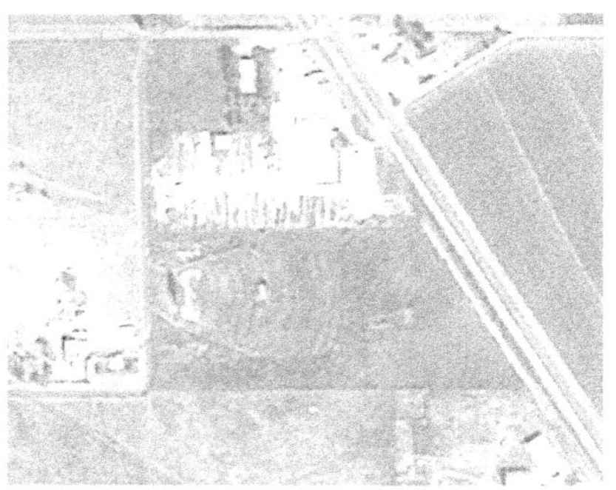

With Poe Street to the north and Highway 256 past the railroad tracks to the east, the Cactus was on a little-used piece of land. October 1975 photo by the New Mexico Department of Transportation.

In March 1974, the Cactus ran an advertisement offering a reward for the conviction of whoever stole its projection equipment. An aerial photo from October 1975 showed the drive-in intact with an east-facing screen. By 1978, a trucking firm on Poe Street had taken over the field behind the projection building, and by 1981, the Cactus was completely gone. The site is now the south end of a recycling center in place of the old trucking firm. The drive-in's entrance connected to today's Kallahin Road.

Jingle Bob Drive-In

Location: Just northeast of town on Country Club Road, where Goddard High School's baseball diamonds are today
Opened: July 31, 1951
Closed: Oct. 15, 1965
Capacity: 500 cars

Theatre Enterprises built the Jingle Bob, named for John Chisum's ranch, right after building the Ballojak. In fact, they must have been building them simultaneously, since they opened just a few days apart in July 1951.

The Jingle Bob may have taken a few years off for some reason. Its ad on July 20, 1956 said, "Jinglebob Drive-In will be closed after Saturday showings". That was an unusual, one-word spelling and an even more unusual mid-summer closing. Future summers came and went without the Jingle Bob.

As with several other New Mexico drive-ins, ownership passed to Frontier Theatres, then to Commonwealth Theatres. Based on its

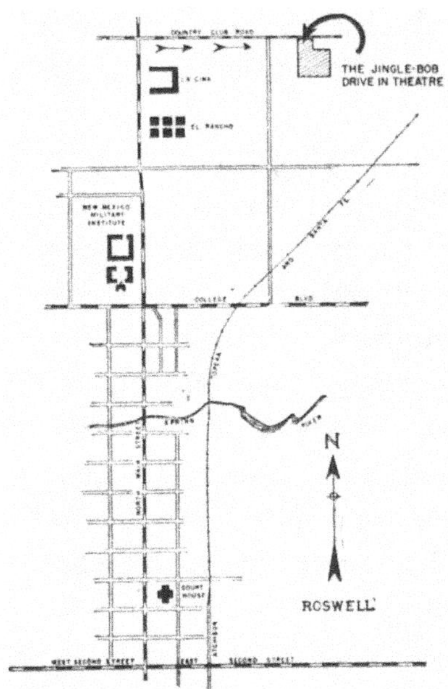

The Jingle Bob's grand opening ad included this handy map.

ads in the *Roswell Daily Record*, the now-hyphenated Jingle-Bob reopened in the summer of 1964. After another two seasons, the drive-in's final ad came in mid-October 1965. The Goddard High School sports complex occupies the site today.

Starlite Drive-In

Location: Southeast of town on US 285 just north of the fairgrounds
Opened: May 18, 1949
Closed: 1984?
Capacity: 450 cars

In August 1948, Theatre Enterprises announced that it was building the Valley Drive-In near the Roswell city limits. It said the foundations were nearly finished, and that they hoped to open the Valley in September. I'm assuming that at some point that project was delayed until spring, and that the Valley was renamed the Starlite, which held its grand opening in May 1949. The drive-in added a second screen in 1955.

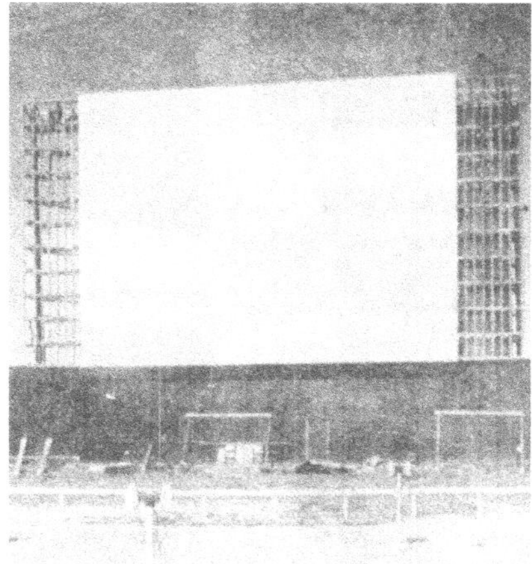

In 1955, the Starlite's owners widened its main screen, as shown in this *Roswell Daily Record* photo. They added a second screen later that year.

In a typical 1956 ad in the *Roswell Daily Record*, the Starlite boasted of a "ferris wheel, merry-go-round, slides, swings and bucking broncos!" Its playground equipment sat in front of the screen.

In 1958, the Starlite was something of a pioneer in the drive-in flea market concept. Unlike most later versions that would operate in mornings and afternoons, the Starlite's "Swap Night" was held on late Friday afternoons from 5:30 until 15 minutes before the movies started.

In the early 1960s, Frontier Theatres bought out Theatre Enterprises, and Commonwealth Theatres bought Frontier's drive-ins in 1968. I'm not sure when the drive-in closed. It was intact in a 1983 aerial photo, and Commonwealth included it in its holdings in the 1984 *Motion Picture Almanac*. The lot remains vacant today with hints of the Starlite's ramps still visible.

Ruidoso

At an elevation of 6900 feet, Ruidoso's status as a mountain resort started with a ski area in 1935. The Hollywood Park horse racing track, named for the

Hollywood neighborhood, opened in 1947, adding to the village's allure as a cooler summer getaway.

Also see: Ruidoso Downs.

Hollywood Drive-In

Location: Somewhere on US 70 in the Hollywood neighborhood
Opened: Aug. 6, 1954
Closed: Sept. 20, 1955
Capacity: 80? cars

The Hollywood Drive-In, in the Hollywood neighborhood on the east side of Ruidoso, was active for two short seasons. The drive-in was built by H. H. Daniels and featured a screen tower with a mural painted by two high school boys. The *Ruidoso News* mentioned that it was on US 70, but I never saw an exact location.

The Hollywood opened on August 6, 1954. An accompanying story in the *News* that day said its ramps could hold about "80 cars"; that may have been a misprint, but it's the only capacity number I've ever found. The drive-in had in-car speakers and a short distance from the projection booth to the screen.

In April 1955, high winds toppled the Hollywood's screen, but Daniels rebuilt it and reopened on May 10. The drive-in's final night was on September 20, 1955. The Daniels family advertised

The top of the Hollywood's grand opening ad as it appeared in the *Ruidoso News*.

the drive-in for sale in both off-seasons. In early 1956, the owners of the competing Mt. Vue Drive-In bought the Hollywood and kept it closed. They sold it along with the Mt. Vue in September 1957.

Probably in reaction to the construction of the nearby Downs Drive-In, in April 1959 the new owners announced they would quickly build another drive-in in Hollywood, but it appears that nothing came of that announcement.

Mt. Vue Drive-In

Location: Just north of town on then-New Mexico 37, where the Sierra Mall is today
Opened: July 1950
Closed: Oct. 30, 1975
Capacity: 250 cars

William Eiland built the "Mt. Vue" (how it was spelled on its sign) Drive-In in 1950. Its first ad in the *Ruidoso News* on July 14 said it was "Now Open," which may have been its grand opening, or not.

In May 1953, Eiland began emphasizing the restaurant angle of his drive-in by adding a cartoon chef and the "Sho-Dyn" (pronounced "show dine") name to its ads. Around the end of the 1957 season, local men Ed Wimberly and Ken Newton bought the Mt. Vue Sho-Dyn from Eiland. For the 1958 season, the new owners built a 12-foot-high neon sign on the highway. For the 1959 season, they added a 240-seat glass-front indoor theater, adding "Indorama" to the drive-in's already complicated name.

In June 1964, Wimberly bought out Newton's share of the Mt. Vue. The drive-in

The name and the graphics were getting complicated at the top of this typical ad for the Mt. Vue Drive-In Sho-Dyn.

continued to operate for another 11 years, closing quietly at the end of the 1975 season. Its final listing in the *Motion Picture Almanac* indicated that J. Yates owned the Mt. Vue, so it may have been sold in its final years. The Sierra Mall, which includes the indoor Sierra Cinema, occupies the site today.

Ruidoso Downs

The city of Ruidoso Downs incorporated in 1947, and the former Hollywood Park race track was renamed Ruidoso Downs a few years later. At 407 residents (per the 1960 census), this was probably the smallest municipality in New Mexico to ever open its own drive-in.

Downs Drive-In

Location: Directly across US 70 from the race track entrance
Opened: May 7, 1959
Closed: Aug. 30, 1976
Capacity: 300 cars

J. C. Capps and Mr. and Mrs. George Westall, owners of the indoor Pueblo Theatre in Ruidoso, built their drive-in in the spring of 1959. Anita Reynolds won the name-the-drive-in contest with the straightforward Downs. It featured a wide screen and a narrow field of eight ramps.

The Downs' final entry in the *Motion Picture Almanac*

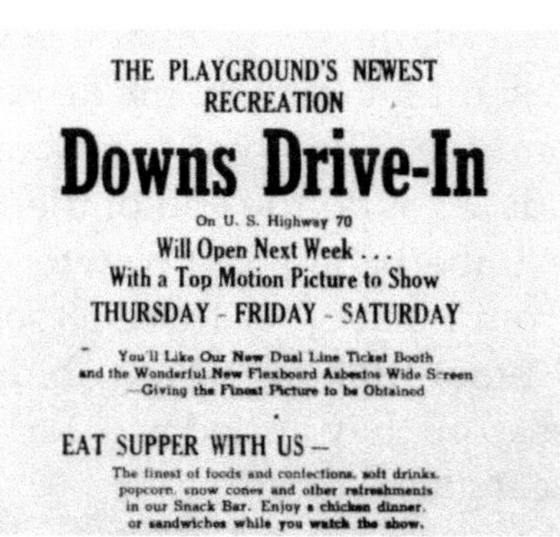

The top and bottom parts of the Downs Drive-In's grand opening ad in the *Ruidoso News,* back when an asbestos screen was a selling point. That mention of US 70 is the only clue I've seen to its exact location.

listed its owner as E. Lemons, so the original owners may have sold the place in its final years. The drive-in's final ad in the *Ruidoso News* appeared at the end of the 1976 season. The Ladera Apartments are there now, though you can see the old entrance and exit paths between the apartments and US 70.

Intermission: Concession Stand Evolution

If you had a chance to visit a drive-in, and I hope you have, you've probably encountered the relatively modern cafeteria-style food and drink setup. But it turns out that it took a lot of changes from the beginning of the drive-in era to get us to where we are now. Changes spurred by the survival of the most profitable. In short, a rapid evolution.

The evolution of movie snack bars starts with indoor theaters. Most of the earliest movie theaters sold no snacks.

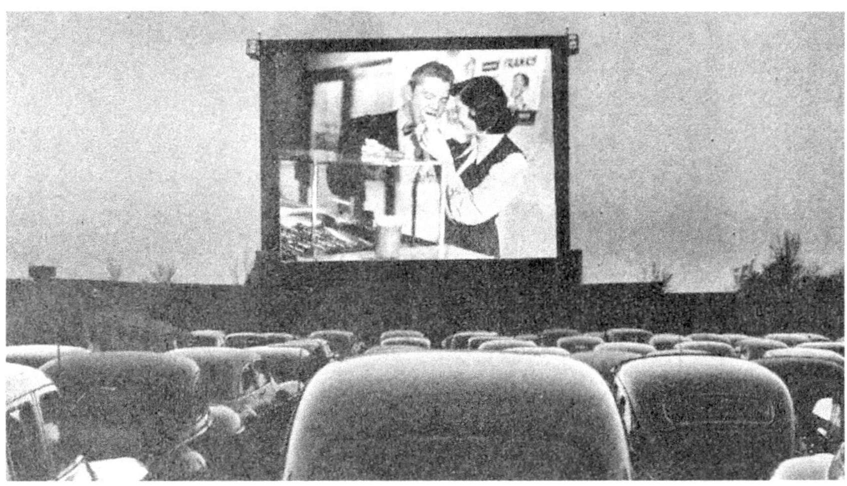

Armour was one of many companies that would provide drive-ins with free concession stand promotional trailers to show during intermission. Soft drink makers such as Coke and Pepsi were more common sponsors in the 1960s and 70s. Photo from the Jan. 10, 1950 *Motion Picture Herald*.

Street vendors popped corn in carts in front of theater entrances; the smell of fresh popcorn was as strong a draw then as it is now. Eventually a few of the smarter theater owners brought the vendors inside, leasing their lobby for a cut of the profits. Before long, even smarter owners set up their own concession stands.

(Remember also that it was difficult to make popcorn at home until the late 1950s. Then the introduction of the stovetop Jiffy Pop and the lesser-known E-Z Pop gave families the only easy way to make fresh popcorn. Before microwave ovens and Jiffy Pop, the opportunity for a popcorn treat provided a special incentive to go to the movies. But I digress.)

When drive-ins started in the 1930s, some of them omitted concession stands entirely. Other early drive-ins contracted with vendors to run the food side of the

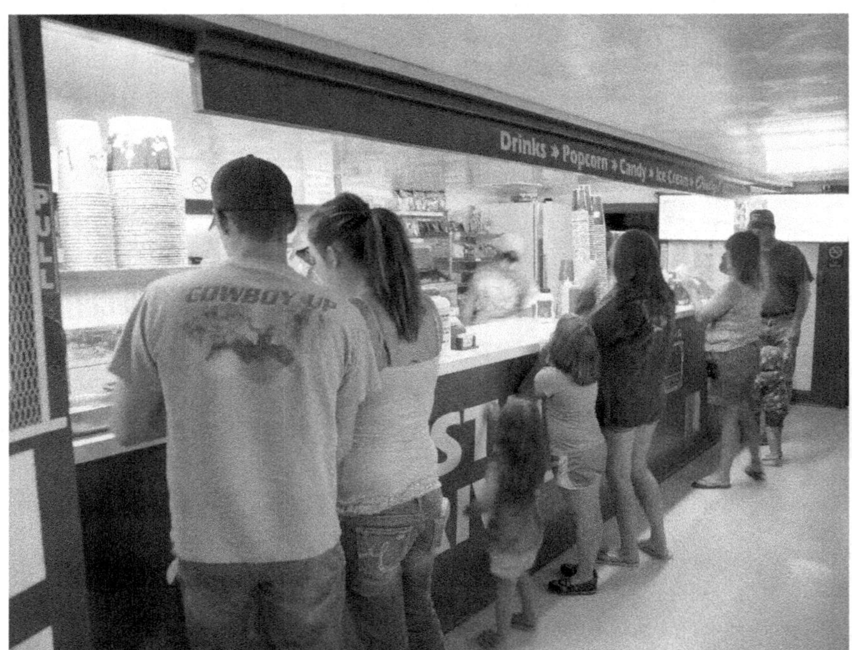

Walk-up concession stands were once common at drive-ins. The Star Drive-In, built in 1950 in Montrose CO, still keeps theirs that way. Photo © Joe Sohm / Dreamstime.com.

business. The practice changed after World War II, when thousands of new drive-ins learned through trial and error which approaches were the most profitable.

First were the stands themselves. The earliest concession stands faced the elements. Customers would walk up, place an order, and a worker would gather the requested items and process payment. More modern drive-ins enclosed the concession stand, usually with air conditioning. Customers could relax inside a climate-controlled atmosphere, encouraging them to linger and buy more.

Next were the movie programs themselves. Many drive-ins started by showing the same movie, plus shorts and a cartoon, twice a night. Operators soon recognized that double features were smarter, since they provided a natural break for selling to a captive audience.

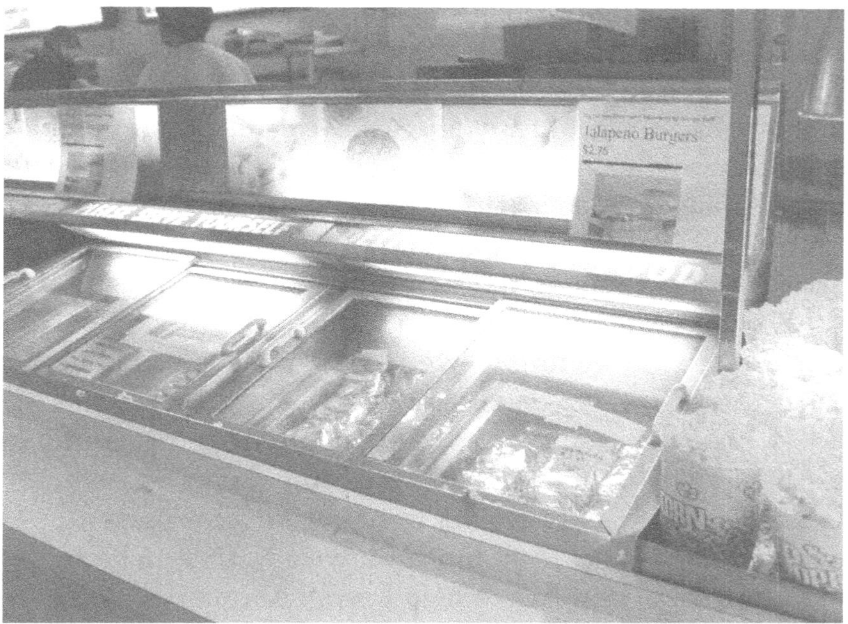

Modern drive-ins switched to efficient cafeteria-style service, with trays on a long slider past prepackaged snacks and sandwiches on the way to a cashier at the end. 2013 photo by the author of the 88 Drive-In, Commerce City CO.

The serving style changed. As much as half of a drive-in's concession volume occurred during intermission, typically 10 minutes. Early experiments with cafeteria-style service spread like wildfire, becoming the norm in just a few years. At the larger drive-ins, patrons would push a tray along a line, adding pre-packaged snacks and drinks as desired, and they pay the cashier at the end.

Another area of change was the menu. Drive-ins originally offered the same snacks as indoor theaters. They soon learned that many of the families who came to the drive-in wanted more than a snack, they wanted a meal. Hamburgers and hot dogs became some of the best sellers. In the 1950s, some drive-ins began offering then-exotic treats such as egg rolls and pizza, sometimes as the only place in town to get that kind of food.

On the other hand, drive-in operators discovered that beyond a certain point, adding food options to the menu resulted in lower profits. Patrons would pause to consider which option to choose, and in the cafeteria format, the line moves only as quickly as its slowest customer.

Priming the drive-in customer to buy was another important job for savvy drive-in owners. Free playgrounds for children were a way to get them and their parents to arrive early and spend more time at the snack bar. And the concession stand trailers shown during intermission preached to the waiting viewers that the tastiest food in town was waiting to be purchased.

Concession stand profits kept many drive-ins going, especially when they sold snacks during daylight swap meets. Today they're an important part of a theater's overall bottom line. Next time you visit a drive-in, be sure to buy a bag of popcorn to help keep them alive.

Santa Fe

The oldest US state capital, named provincial capital in 1610, has so much history and art. Both intersect downtown at some of my favorite places, the Santa Fe Plaza and the Palace of the Governors. Santa Fe is probably the largest city to have seen Route 66 abandon it; the 1937 rerouting in New Mexico bypassed it.

Also see: Tesuque.

Pueblo Drive-In

Location: About a mile southwest of town on then-US 85, now Cerrillos Road
Opened: May 29, 1958
Closed: Sept. 14, 1980
Capacity: 500 cars

Way back in 1950, as they were nearing completion of their first drive-in in Tesuque, Greer Enterprises announced plans to build another "on the Albuquerque road shortly beyond the city limits." That's a good description of the future location of the Pueblo Drive-In, which was effectively moved from Tesuque eight years later. The new location was just southwest of town, a mile away from its competitor, the Yucca.

Greer built a new, curved 40x80-foot screen, a new snack bar, and a new playground. They also expanded the viewing field

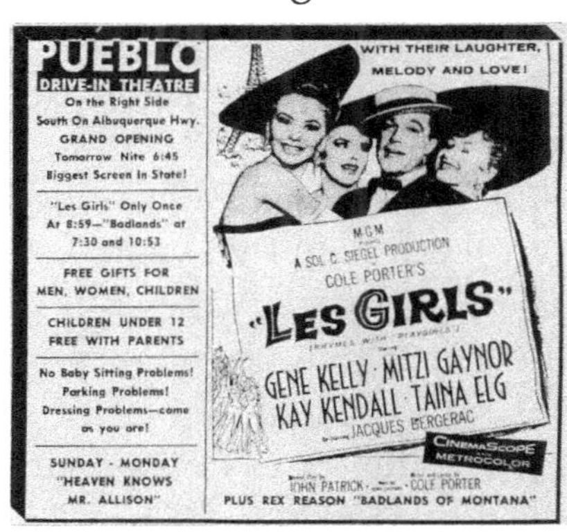

The Pueblo's grand opening ad gave no clue that the drive-in had shifted from Tesuque about 11 miles away.

from 400 to 500 cars. It makes me wonder whether they at least brought the original marquee to the new site.

In October 1962, Greer sold its four Santa Fe theaters to Frontier Theaters. Commonwealth bought out Frontier's drive-ins in 1968. That's the company that ran the Pueblo for the rest of its life, quietly closing it after the 1980 season. In 1985, the Pueblo was torn down to make way for a Walmart, which still occupies the site today.

Yucca Drive-In

Location: About two miles southwest of town on then-US 85, now Cerrillos Road
Opened: July 4, 1950
Closed: Oct. 30, 1994
Capacity: 500 cars

Charles Brent, a veteran of 30 years in show business in Texas and Oklahoma, spent over $100,000 to build the Yucca in 1950. It featured a children's playground, black-topped ramps, landscaping with sprinklers, and the new cafeteria-style snack bar that he called a "concessi-teria." Brent would put on stage shows twice a week on the roof of the concession stand.

Less than two years after it opened, Brent sold the Yucca to Richard Wiles & Brooks Noah, who also owned the Pines Drive-In in Excelsior Springs MO. Asked in 1994 why two Missouri men would buy a New Mexico drive-in, Wiles

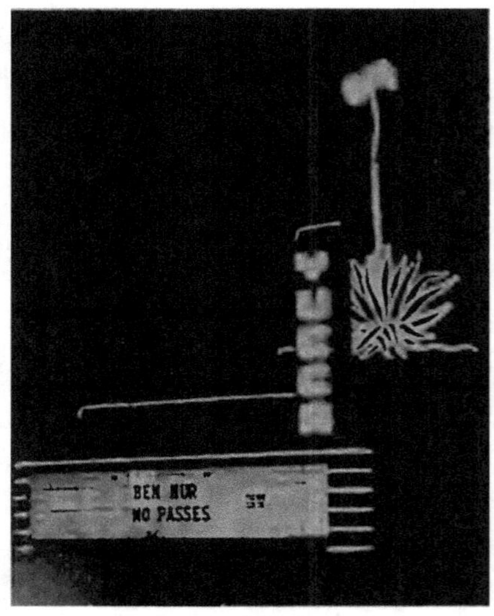

This rare look at the Yucca sign at night was published by *Boxoffice* in 1963.

remembered, "Well, it was for sale." The new owners widened the Yucca's screen in 1955.

A *Boxoffice* feature in 1963 said the Yucca's 550-foot frontage was lined with six-foot redwood fencing. The sides and back were fenced with barbed wire. Blue lights on 60-foot poles lit the viewing field during the movie. At intermission, two lights on the screen plus white lights on the poles provided plenty of illumination for patrons to find the snack bar.

Wiles and Noah kept the Yucca into the mid-1980s. Around 1985, three high school girls died in a terrible auto accident while leaving the theater. Wiles suffered a stroke in 1987, then gave the Yucca property in a charitable trust to Concordia College of Moorhead MN. Jonathan Kahn of Trans-Lux Southwest stepped in and took over the drive-in, leasing it on a year-to-year basis from the college.

Concordia put the drive-in up for sale in 1994, so everyone knew it was the Yucca's final season. It closed with the 1948 film *Sitting Pretty*, one of the movies it showed on its first night. Kahn said at the time that Trans-Lux would keep the Yucca's sign in storage, "hopefully to use with a new theater." Concordia netted more than $3 million from the sale. The Yucca's screen was demolished a couple of years later, though the lot remained vacant for a decade. A bank and a condominium occupy the site today.

Santa Rosa

Thanks to the Blue Hole, an 81-foot-deep natural well, Santa Rosa is known as 'The Scuba Diving Capital of the Southwest." The city's "Fat Man" cartoon portrait, originally for the Club Café and rescued in 1991 by Joseph's Bar and Grill, has been a Route 66 landmark since 1935.

Sky-Ranch Drive-In

Location: On the west side of town on US 54 less than half a mile south of US 66
    Opened: Aug. 15, 1952
    Closed: 1962?
    Capacity: 200 cars

In the 1930s, Lester Dollison put together a little circuit of indoor theaters, mostly in Texas. By 1944, he was running the Studio in Vaughn NM, about 40 miles from Santa Rosa, and he enjoyed the cooler evenings there. In 1948, Dollison bought the Pecos in Santa Rosa. He also opened a couple of drive-ins elsewhere, including the Skyway in Amarillo TX, before turning to southwest Santa Rosa.

On the day the Sky-Ranch opened, the pages of the *Santa Rosa News* were dominated by a different new facility, Guadalupe General Hospital. The grand opening notice for the drive-in, on the back pages, boasted a "mammoth screen." The *Theatre Catalog* later listed the "Sky Ranch" (no hyphen) with a capacity of 200 cars, though *Motion Picture Almanac* pegged its capacity at 250.

The Sky-Ranch looked intact in a 1962 aerial photo, but a May 1962 issue of the *News* included only the Pecos, with no mention of a drive-in. Dollison stayed in

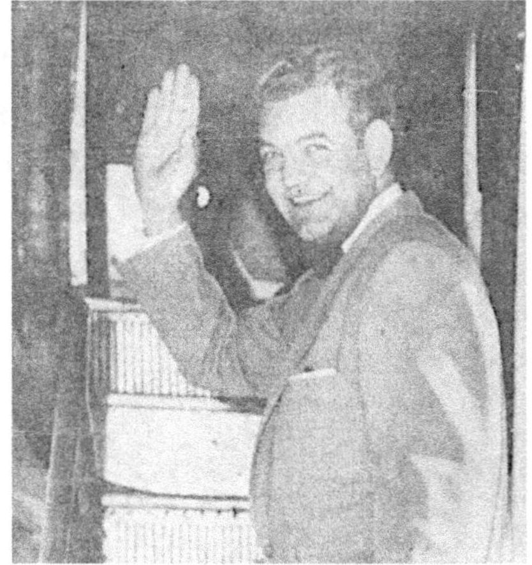

We're run into Sky-Ranch owner Lester Dollison often enough in this book that I thought I'd provide a picture of him. In this 1954 photo from the *Austin Statesman*, Les is about to be Pioneer Airlines' millionth passenger.

Santa Rosa for a while, renaming the Pecos as the Rodeo in 1965, but there were never any other mentions of the Sky-Ranch. Although it was still intact in a 1973 photo, the screen was gone by 1983. Today scattered housing occupies the site, just north of the new Guadalupe County Hospital.

Shiprock

Named for a nearby rock formation, Shiprock was founded in 1903 on the Navajo reservation by an agent of the US Bureau of Indian Affairs. Today it's a census-designated place holding about 7700 residents.

Chief Drive-In

Location: On then-US 666, now US 491, about a quarter mile north of its intersection with then-US 550, now US 64
Opened: December? 1954
Closed: 1975?
Capacity: 189 cars

George R. Armstrong, who owned the Arroyo Drive-In just across the border in Cortez CO, said that his new project in Shiprock would be the first drive-in ever built on land owned by Native Americans. That's why he named it the Chief. *Boxoffice* wrote in November 1954 that the Armstrong's drive-in was under construction, and *Variety* said in January 1955

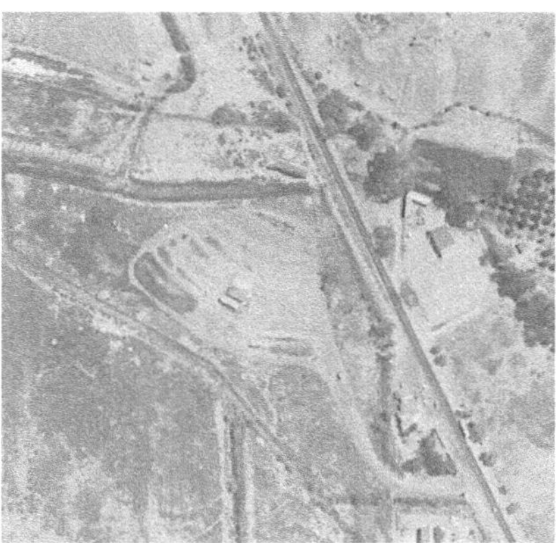

This 1961 photo by the New Mexico Department of Transportation suggests that the Chief's screen was separated from the viewing field by a stream or gully.

that the Chief had opened, so I'll guess that the true opener was around December.

Armstrong, then a deputy district attorney, still owned the Chief in June 1957, when his name hit the *Denver Post* because of an apparently unrelated tax issue. The theater advertised only occasionally in the *Farmington Daily Times*, including at least once in 1959.

The Chief's ownership beyond Armstrong is a big muddle to me. In the summer of 1960, Claude Marques took out a loan using the Chief as collateral, possibly to buy the drive-in. In February 1961, William and Ruby Daniel, the lenders, took possession of the Chief and advertised an auction of its assets. Later in 1961, while filing for bankruptcy, Marques told a U.S. District Court that he had operated the Chief from June 1960 to February 1961. In his frequently accurate booklet *Sodas & Shows*, regional historian Zang Wood wrote that the Chief closed in the early 1960s, then Allen Theaters took over and reopened it in 1966.

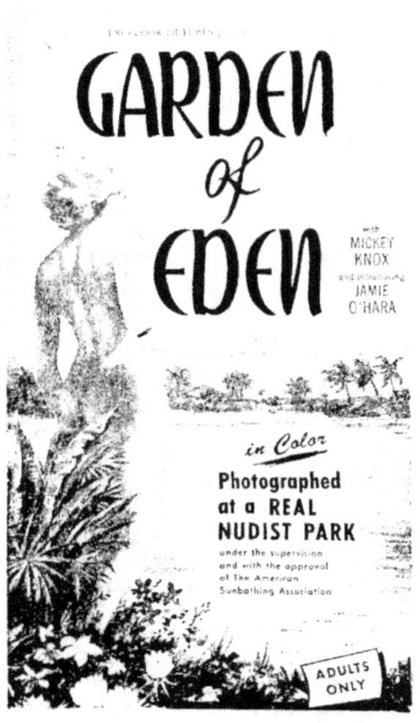

The Chief didn't advertise very often in the *Farmington Daily Times*. When it did, it was often for special occasions such as this. (And I love the juxtaposition of "Adults Only" with the reduced rate for children.)

Wood wrote about several altercations with unhappy neighbors and patrons. "Due to these types of incidents, the resentment of some tribal members, declining revenues, the difficulty in hiring employees, the time and distance required to keep it open, the decision was made to close down the theater in 1975." The *Motion Picture Almanac*'s 1977 edition showed the Chief still owned by Allen, but it may have been slow to notice the closure. By 1979, a *Daily Times* article called it the "old Chief Drive-In."

The Shiprock Area Community Cleanup in June 1988 was supposed to include "the old Chief Drive-In sign's demolition." However, in March 1989, the Shiprock Indian Health Hospital was granted permission "to use the old billboard at Chief Drive-In for public health messages." The billboard is gone today, and the old Chief site is vacant with no trace of the drive-in remaining.

Silver City

On July 21, 1895, heavy rains caused a deluge of water to flood and wash out young Silver City's Main Street, leaving a 55-foot-deep ditch in its place. The businesses there switched their entrances to Bullard Street in back, and the former Main Street became Big Ditch Park, still delighting visitors today.

Also see: Arenas Valley.

Silver Sky-Vue Drive-In

Location: About a mile east of town on US 180
Opened: 1953?
Closed: Aug. 17, 1974
Capacity: 225 cars

The Silver Sky-Vue is a rare example of a drive-in whose closing I know more about than its opening. In June

1952, former Paramount salesman Steve Ward said that he and some friends would build a Silver City drive-in. In November 1952, the guys who had just opened the Copper Drive-In a few miles down the road said they would build another drive-in closer to town. As far as I can tell, nothing came from either of those announcements.

H. D. McCloughan, who owned a few other theaters in the region, began building Silver City's drive-in in the summer of 1953. At the time, it was to be named the Silver. (Although other sources spelled it several ways, McCloughan later wrote the drive-in's name, Silver Sky-Vue, with a hyphen and an 'e'.)

The Silver Sky-Vue was definitely in operation by April 1954, when McCloughan made regional news by stating he would book the then-controversial movie *Salt of the Earth* at the Silver Sky-Vue. In 1961, McCloughan advertised that the drive-in was for sale. By 1965, it had been purchased by Silco Theatres, run by Lowell Cain.

In April 1968, Cain closed the indoor Gila Theatre in Silver City, saying he'd show its first-run movies at the Silver Sky-Vue. Les Dollison, who owned the Copper by then, swooped in and took over the Gila.

In April 1971, Cain sold the Silver Sky-Vue to U. A. Kane of El Paso. Kane added a second screen, which opened in August that year. Despite his investment, Kane sold the drive-in's land to a shopping center developer in August 1974. A big box store, currently Harbor Freight, sits where the viewing field had been.

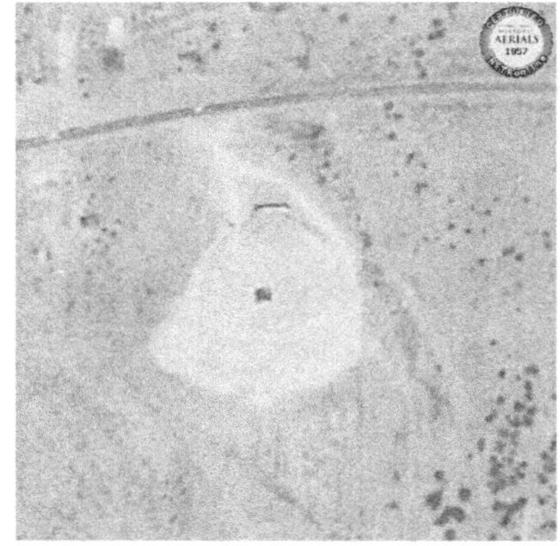

The Silver Sky-Vue's driveways look unpaved in this 1957 photo. © HistoricAerials.com, used by permission.

Socorro

The New Mexico School of Mines, now the New Mexico Institute of Mining and Technology, was founded in Socorro in 1889. Just west of the campus is the New Mexico Tech Golf Course, home of the target for the longest hole I've heard of, the Elfego Baca Golf Shoot, an annual event where contestants tee off from the top of "M" Mountain, three miles away, 2600 feet up.

Sunset / Star-Lite Drive-In

Location: On a 600x600-foot plot somewhere around Socorro
Opened: March? 1949
Closed: 1950?
Capacity: 100 cars

I'm sure that the tiny Sunset Drive-In briefly existed in Socorro, but I don't know where. It was built by Edsel Cavasos, who started his drive-in with 100 in-car speakers and promised to add more when needed, according to a note in the March 26, 1949 issue of *Boxoffice*.

Just 11 weeks later, Cavasos was advertising the Sunset for sale in a *Boxoffice* classified ad. "100-car drive-in with in-car speakers. Up and coming town of 6,000. Only one small theatre in town. New Mexico School of Mines located in town; 600x600 ft. plot on which theatre is built is leased with good, long lease. $6,500. Sunset Drive-In, Socorro, N. M."

The next few *Boxoffice* notes raise as many questions as they answer. On Oct. 8, 1949, it reported that "Owner Jack Wills says that weather conditions and construction difficulty have made it impossible to reopen the local drive-in this season. Three attempts have been made previously to complete remodeling of the theatre." Wills owned the indoor Loma Theatre in Socorro.

In July 22, 1950, *Boxoffice* wrote about a projection booth fire at the "Star-Lite Drive-In" in Socorro, "owned and operated by Edsell Casavos. (sic)" Three weeks later, the magazine said that "Casavos has rebuilt the projection booth, replaced missing speakers, and installed new projectors." That's the last note I could find about this drive-in. Cavasos opened a radio/TV repair shop in Hatch but passed away in 1957 at the age of 36.

100-car drive-in with in-car speakers. Up and cuming town of 6,000. Only one small theatre in town. New Mexico School of Mines located in town; 600x600 ft. plot on which theatre is built is leased with good, long lease. $6,500. Sunset Drive-In, Socorro, N. M.

This ad in the "Theatres For Sale" classifieds of the June 11, 1949 issue of *Boxffice* is the best evidence that the Sunset existed in Socorro.

The reference to the School of Mines in the for-sale ad guarantees that we're talking about the same place, but where in or near Socorro was that 600x600 plot? I've stared at blurry aerial photos from the period, and all I can tell is that it definitely wasn't the site of the future Sierra Drive-In. What was Wills' involvement, and what was that remodeling/reopening stuff about? Why did the Sunset change its name to the Star-Lite? I just wish I knew more about Socorro's first drive-in.

Sierra / Sierra Vista Drive-In

Location: About a mile south of town on then-US 85, now New Mexico 1

Opened: April 24, 1952

Closed: 1987?

Capacity: 400 cars

Socorro's second drive-in was much more conventional than its first. Supervised by theater engineer George Frantz, Gibraltar Theatres built the 200-car Sierra

Drive-In in early 1952. Five years later, Gibraltar sold the Sierra to Les Dollison.

It looks like the Sierra closed for a while. A 1971 USGS aerial photo showed the concession building intact but the screen gone. Dollison rejuvenated the drive-in in 1978, holding a naming contest. The winning entry was Sierra Vista, almost the same as the original. The refurbished drive-in held its "grand opening" that fall.

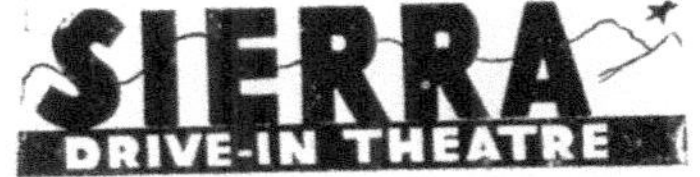

This grand opening ad appeared the day before in the *Socorro Chieftain.*

It had room for at least 400 cars, all facing a 35x70-foot metal screen. The sound system was new, and the snack bar refreshed.

I'm not sure when the Sierra Vista closed. In August 1988, drive-in movie columnist Joe Bob Briggs wrote, "The Sierra Vista, last drive-in in Socorro, N.M., is evidently closed for good." The screen and projection building are still standing today.

Spencerville

Spencerville is a census-designated place that's home to more than a thousand people. It sits on NM 516 about three miles west of Aztec. It was named for Clark Spencer, a farmer who lived nearby. In 1940, Spencer told the US Census that his occupation was bricklayer, so maybe his farm didn't survive the Dust Bowl.

Yucca Drive-In

Location: One block north of then-US 550, now-New Mexico 516, about four miles east of Farmington
Opened: May 1, 1958
Closed: Sept. 26, 1959
Capacity: 200 cars

In the 1957-58 offseason, there was something of a race in the Farmington area to build another drive-in. Porter Smith, who owned the Rincon in Aztec, partnered with Paul Campbell on one project. Russell Allen and Kelly Crawford, owners of Farmington's Apache and Valley, announced they would build the 986-car Oasis. Smith and Campbell won the race, opening the Yucca in May 1958. I suspect that Allen and Crawford reevaluated how many drive-ins the region would support; the Oasis never opened.

The Yucca operated for just two seasons, closing quietly in the last week of September 1959. At least, it never ran another movie ad in the *Farmington Daily Times*.

Was that really when the Yucca closed for good? In his booklet *Sodas & Shows*, local historian Zang Wood wrote that "in late 1958 (sic) a very strong wind blew down the screen. Business was in decline due to the economy slump and the rise of television. As a result the decision was made not to rebuild." On the other hand, a 1962 aerial photo showed the Yucca and its screen still intact, and a January 1963 *Daily Times* classified ad gave directions as "east of

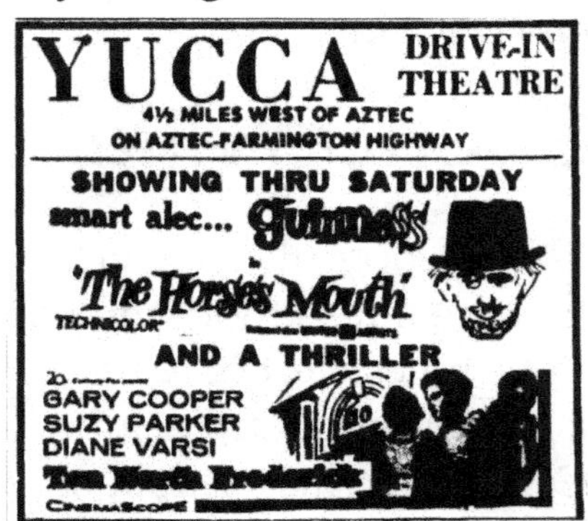

The Yucca's final ad in the *Farmington Daily Times*.

Yucca drive-in theatre." The lot was vacant by 1981. Storage units occupy the site today.

Taos

The American flag flies day and night in Taos Plaza. That tradition started during the Civil War, when Unionists Kit Carson and Smith Simpson raised the flag and guarded it against Confederate sympathizers. Taos claims to be the first place to continuously fly the Stars and Stripes.

Kit Carson Drive-In

Location: Over a mile southwest of town on then-US 64, now New Mexico 68
Opened: May? 1956
Closed: Sept. 1, 1984
Capacity: 365 cars

Henry Ford Taylor built the Kit Carson Drive-In in the spring of 1956. At the time, it was described as having a capacity of 247 or 300 cars, depending on the source. It apparently opened around Memorial Day that year.

In 1957, a bolt of lightning hit the Kit Carson, digging a ditch up to three feet deep in spots. A bulldozer put the ramps back in shape for the show that night.

Taylor sold the Kit Carson in the first week of June 1962, days after receiving a cancer diagnosis. He died on August 25 that

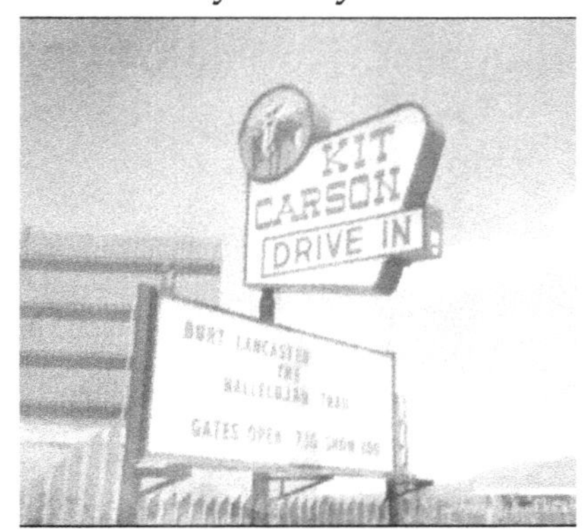

Circa 1965 photo by Anthony L. Vazquez-Hernandez via CinemaTreasures.org.

year. The buyer was the family of William Beutler, grandson of Taos Art Colony founder Bert Phillips.

In the spring of 1964, a strong wind toppled the Kit Carson's screen. Beutler reopened the indoor Taos Theatre, under repair at the time, during the weeks it took to rebuild the drive-in screen.

Regional theater mogul Les Dollison bought the Kit Carson in March 1970. He ran it for the rest of its life, selling it in September 1984 to Walmart, which still occupies the site today.

Tatum

James G. Tatum opened a store in 1909 and brought his neighbors their mail from Scott until he was granted a post office of his own. Today, in the middle of town, Poor Boy's Metal Art shows off an amazing array of monkeys hanging from trees, cowboys on the range, and a metal version of the Iwo Jima statue.

Coyote Drive-In

Location: Over a mile south of town on then-New Mexico 18, now NM 206
Opened: November? 1952
Closed: 1974?
Capacity: 300 cars

Texan Estes Burgamy and R. A. Daniels of Tatum, who bought the indoor Tatum Theatre in February 1952, built the town's only drive-in later that year. In July, *Motion Picture Herald* wrote that it was due to open on August 15. However, the first mention I could find in the *Lovington Leader* was on Nov. 4, when Tatum's local electrician was "rewiring the Coyote Drive-Inn". The first Coyote ad in the *Leader* appears to have been

Nov. 7, with no mention of a grand opening.

Daniels and his son H. H. built the short-lived Hollywood Drive-In in Ruidoso two years later. In April 1962, the Coyote held its first Easter service. And that's about all I know.

The *Motion Picture Almanac* always listed Burgamy as the Coyote's sole owner. When the MPA rebooted its drive-in list in

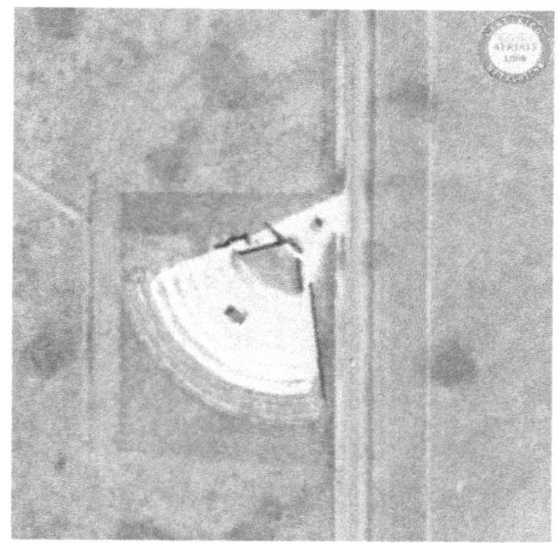

The Coyote was still in great shape in this 1968 photo. © HistoricAerials.com, used by permission.

the 1977 edition, the Coyote was gone. I don't know what year the drive-in closed. A 1968 aerial photo showed the Coyote still intact, but the screen was gone by 1983. The projection building still stands at the site along with the ridge that used to support the Coyote's screen.

Tesuque

Just north of Tesuque, a census-designated place named for the nearby Tesuque Pueblo, you'll find Camel Rock. The 40-foot-high formation of pinkish-tan sandstone is called that because, well, it looks just like a kneeling camel.

Pueblo Drive-In

Location: On then-US 84, now NM-591, about 6½ miles north of Santa Fe, just outside Tesuque
Opened: June 9, 1950
Closed: Sept. 28, 1957
Capacity: 500 cars

E. John Greer, the president of Santa Fe theaters owner Salmon-Greer, Inc., went all out in building the Pueblo Drive-In a few miles out of town in Tesuque. In addition to moonlight lighting, "new ideas in concession bars," and "children's amusements," the Pueblo featured a 44-foot screen tower. Navajo artist Quincy Tahoma painted a mural on its back of a warrior on a rearing horse spooked by a skunk.

The opening date for the $75,000 project kept slipping. When it was first announced, the target date was April. By March, it had moved to May. It finally opened in June. That year, Pueblo manager Tom Pillsbury would grab a microphone during the intermissions to ask patrons to turn on their headlights if they were enjoying the show.

The drive-in's location was fairly remote. One moviegoer later remembered, "The strongest memory for me is the pungent smell of Russian olives [trees] and the sound of bull frogs across the road."

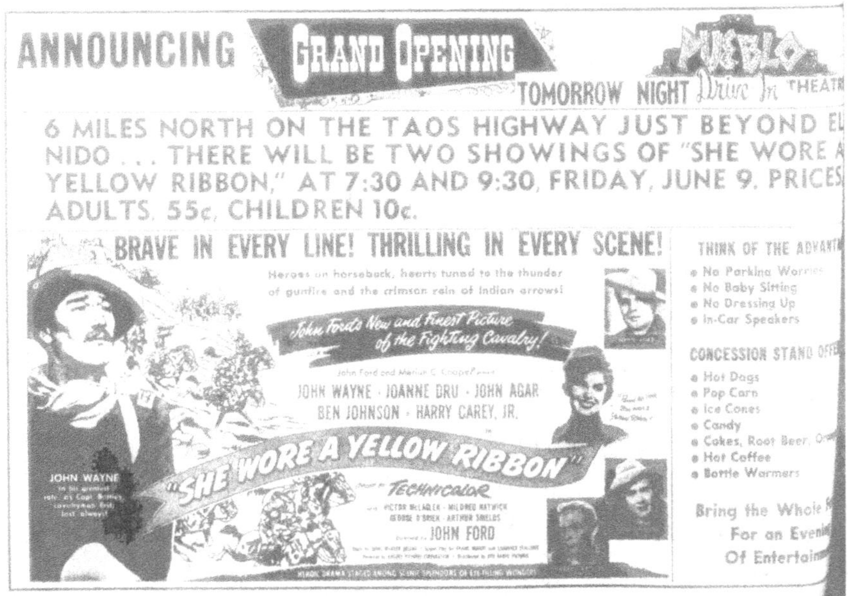

The Pueblo's grand opening ad in the *Santa Fe New Mexican* provided a lot of information about the drive-in.

Greer passed away in 1952, leaving his three sons in charge of the business. A few years later, they got the idea to move the Pueblo closer to Santa Fe, where the Yucca Drive-In was doing good business. In its final ad in September 1957, they wrote, "The Pueblo will close Sat. nite for the season. Thank you for your patronage and we hope to see you next year." The next time the Pueblo opened, it was a mile away from the Yucca. At the original location, only faint traces of the ramps remain today.

Truth or Consequences

See Williamsburg.

Tucumcari

The city promoted itself with "Tucumcari tonight" billboards along Route 66, promising decent rooms in otherwise sparsely populated eastern New Mexico. Among the most impressive survivors of that time are the Blue Swallow Motel, a gorgeous facility built in 1939, and the Motel Safari, filled with Route 66 memorabilia.

Canal Drive-In

Location: About two miles west of town on then-US 66, now US 54
Opened: April 20, 1951
Closed: July 4, 1972
Capacity: 550 cars and 250 seats

Longtime Tucumcari exhibitor Milas Hurley couldn't have been happy when an out-of-town entrepreneur built the city's first drive-in. Hurley didn't rush to respond, eventually choosing his own drive-in site farther west of town, starting construction in September 1950. The Canal, named for the Conchas Canal that formed the site's southern border, was supposed to open on March 25, Easter Sunday, but its grand opening ad in the *Tucumcari News* didn't appear until almost a month later.

The Canal held 550 cars, and its concession stand included a small auditorium to seat about 200 patrons "in case of stormy or cold weather." The manager lived in an on-site apartment with a switch to light up the viewing field if he heard shenanigans in the night.

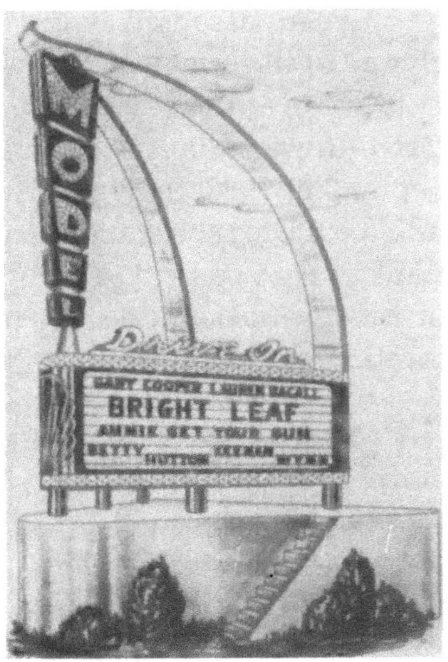

Before the Canal opened, *Motion Picture Herald* reported that its owner had chosen this model of sign.

The whole site was surrounded by a stone wall, giving it an unusual appearance of permanence. Poblocki and Sons of Milwaukee delivered and installed its 30-foot-high sign.

Hurley, who was once president of the New Mexico Theatre Association, seemed to know what he was doing. The Canal prospered as its competition, the County Drive-In, struggled through ownership changes and reboots. In 1963, Hurley sold all of his Tucumcari theaters to Frontier Theatres. Six years later, Commonwealth Theatres bought out the Frontier chain. Commonwealth owned the Canal for the rest of its life, which wasn't all that long. The drive-in dropped out of the *News'* theater ads in the first week of July 1972.

Although a truck stop initially replaced the Canal, the site sits vacant today, without a trace of the drive-in that spent two decades there.

County / No Name Drive-In

Location: On the west side of town on then-US 66
Opened: Oct. 29, 1948
Closed: 1957?
Capacity: 400 cars

John Hasten Snow, who owned and operated the two indoor theaters in Hinton OK, decided in 1948 to build his first drive-in in Tucumcari, over 300 miles west. He started relatively late in the year, which explains why the County Drive-In didn't open until almost the end of October. From the start, it boasted 400 individual speakers and a wide concession-projection building.

Snow reopened the County for the 1949 season, but Loren Yessler owned the place by the start of the 1950 season. My other notes about Loren showed him working in garages in Amarillo TX, but his wife, Bertha Yessler, was postmaster of Nara Visa NM. Bertha was later appointed justice of the peace there – the first woman to hold that position in state history.

Back to the County. Local man Waldo Slusher bought the drive-in, but probably not its land, around 1952. A few years later, Slusher moved to California. Arthur Salcido bought the County from him before the 1954 season. However, Salcido's County ran into financial difficulties in 1955 and appears to have closed in mid-season.

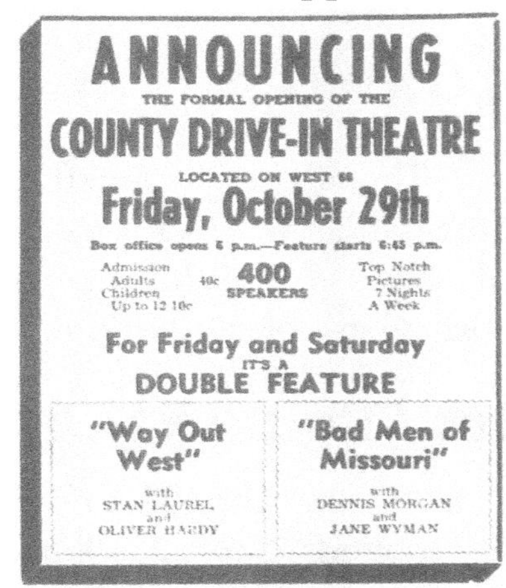

John Hasten Snow, usually called "J.H.," took out a sizeable ad in the *Tucumcari News* to promote the County's grand opening. He sold the drive-in four years later.

The No Name Drive-In, "formerly the County Drive-In / under new management," began advertising in the *Tucumcari News* in August 1956. Those ads continued into 1957, which might be when the drive-in closed for good. In March 1960, Tucumcari's school board voted to buy 32 acres of "the Yessler property" for a new high school, which began construction weeks later on the east side of the land. In 1979, New Mexico authorized a vocational school in Tucumcari, and they built the future Mesalands Community College where the County's viewing field had been.

No Name Drive-In Theatre
(Formerly County Drive-In)
UNDER NEW MANAGEMENT

Tonite and Saturday

BIG **3** SHOWS

1 "Abbott and Costello Meet Dr. Jekyle and Mr. Hyde" With Boris Karloff
AND

2 "The Black Shield of Falsworth"—With Tony Curtis and Janet Leigh
AND

3 Special 30-Minute Cartoon Carnival at 8:33 Free Suckers for the Kids

Gate Opens at 6:15
Dr. Jekyl at 7:15 and 10:53
Carton Carnival at 8:33
Black Shield of Falsworth at

I wish I knew what ownership change led to the County becoming the No Name.

Tularosa

The village is named for Tularosa Creek, derived from the Spanish words for its reddish cattails. Every year on Christmas Eve, it lines US 54 with luminarias, paper bags with a base of sand and a lit candle.

Jet / Route 54 Drive-In

Location: About 1½ miles north of town on US 54
Opened: March 5, 1955
Closed: 1973?
Capacity: 250 cars

If I could find back issues of a Tularosa newspaper, I'd have a lot more information to relay about its drive-in. As it is, we've got some decent hints. Thanks to a later note in the *Alamogordo Daily News*, we know the opening date for Ed Turner's Jet Drive-In. Turner had owned the indoor Muse-U Theater there for eight years when the Jet opened. He was a city councilman at the time, though he resigned in May 1956 after a political spat with the mayor. But I digress.

In 1963, Turner sold the Jet along with the indoor Bijou and Muse-U to Juan and Jose Contreras. Just two years later, Cliff and Susan Reed bought the Muse-U and Jet from the Otero County State Bank.

A season opening ad for the renamed (?) Route 54 from the *Alamogordo Daily News*.

Then it gets a little weird. The often-incorrect *Motion Picture Almanac* listed two Tularosa drive-ins in its 1966 edition – the Jet, owned by R. P. Whitaker, and the Route 54, owned by "R&R Dist." Based on my experience with the *MPA*, this probably meant that the lone drive-in's name had changed. That guess matches a *Daily News* "Gala Opening" ad for the Route 54 Drive-In in September 1966. It described its location as one mile north of Tularosa on US 54, so the Route 54 was probably the renamed Jet. The drive-in offered free dancing nightly before the movies, at least for a while.

That's the last I know about the Route 54. A 1973 aerial photo showed it intact, and in 1984 the screen was up but other small buildings littered the old viewing field. Only the projection building foundation remains today.

Williamsburg

Williamsburg is a small village adjacent to Truth or Consequences, which changed its name from Hot Springs in 1950 to match that of a nationally popular radio show. Ralph Edwards, the show's host, visited "ToC," as it's frequently written, during the first weekend of May for the next 50 years.

Palms / Jet / Palms Drive-In

Location: About two miles south of Truth or Consequences on then-US 85, now NM 187
Opened: July 12, 1951
Closed: Dec. 11, 1971
Capacity: 356 cars

I've written the life stories of hundreds of drive-ins, and I casually know at least a thousand. Of all of those, Williamsburg had the only drive-in that was renamed, then switched back to its original name.

The story of the Palms is the story of James Oscar Conwell. In 1941, he was an electrician advertising in the *Albuquerque Tribune*. Suffering from arthritis, he began visiting the Truth of Consequences (ToC) area seeking relief in its hot mineral waters. By 1951, he had asked the National Production Authority for permission to build a drive-in. After plans at one location fell through, he switched to the eventual Palms site.

When it opened, the Palms used in-car speakers. It had a snack bar and ushers for directing traffic. In 1956, Conwell widened the screen for CinemaScope films. In Albuquerque, Conwell continued his electrician business.

There followed a few years of incomplete information. The drive-in (still?) advertised in the *Hot Springs Herald* as

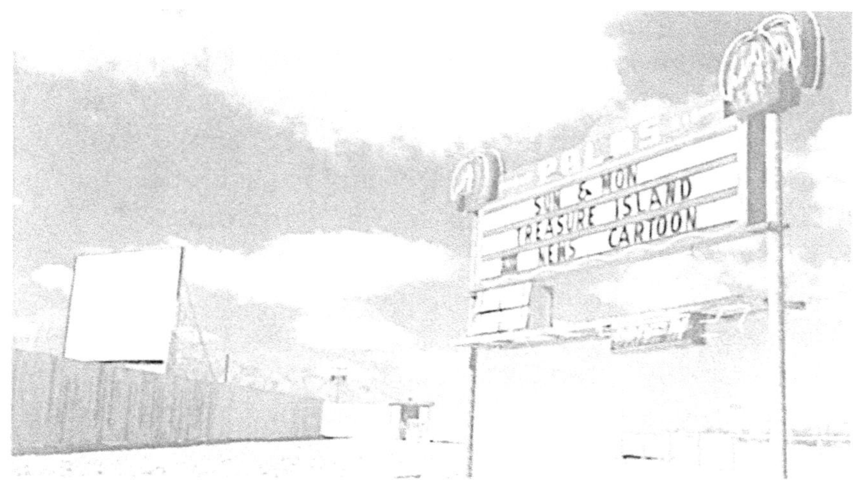

The Palms included this photo in an ad in the 1952 Hot Springs High School yearbook, *The Cub*. I wonder what happened to the sign during those years it was renamed the Jet.

the Palms in the summer of 1958. But by the summer of 1961, classified ads in industry magazines called ToC's drive-in the Jet. Carl Halberg, then owner of two Albuquerque drive-ins, took over the Jet at the start of the 1962 season. Then in February 1964, *Boxoffice* wrote that W. H. McRae had begun operating the Jet, "and it will now be known as the Palms Drive-In."

William O. Hughes ran the Palms starting in April 1965, and ads for the drive-in ran in the *ToC Herald* occasionally through December 1967. The Palms stayed closed for the 1968 summer season, but was acquired by Lucas Graywolf, who refurbished and reopened it that fall.

It was Frank Lasky and Bill Miller's turn in November 1969. They purchased the Palms from Conwell (remember him?), and said they would reopen it in January after remodeling. In May 1970, Lasky sued Miller, so that partnership must have had issues. Whoever was running the drive-in, a *Herald* ad on July 2, 1970 said the Palms was "Now open," and it advertised regularly through December 1971.

In the spring of 1972, Conwell ran classified ads in the *Herald* and the *Tribune*. "For Sale By Owner – Palms Drive In Theatre … Good 40 x 70 ft. screen. 24 ft x 72 ft. block bldg. Projection room, Rest Rooms, Snack bar and store room. Good 8 in. water well. Ticket office, marquee, 180 car spaces plus additional space, 9.52 acres total. $35,000. Would consider terms, of $5,000 down or more." As far as I can tell, the Palms never reopened.

Meanwhile, the *Motion Picture Almanac* had a different story, probably based on outdated data. I mention it only because it adds the name of an interesting character. For its 1962-65 editions, the *MPA* listed the Jet as owned by Coy Zeigler. He was the former owner of at least two Albuquerque businesses, Central Neon Sign and Ceneco Recording. I'd guess that Zeigler either preceded or followed Halberg in the chronological list of owners.

But I should probably call that the list of operators. It seems likely that Conwell always owned the drive-in, probably selling it on his own credit like a used car lot. There's a house on the old Palms lot today, though behind it, the original projection-concession building still stands.

The End

As far as I can tell, there were no New Mexico drive-in theaters in communities that come alphabetically after Williamsburg. Sorry, Winston, Youngsville, and Zuzax.

On the other hand, we'll never reach the end to these stories. There are newspaper clippings and scrapbooks out there that can fill in some of the missing pieces of these histories, and occasionally correct them. If you've got them, drop an email to mkilgore@carload.com.

Bonus materials, new information, and yes, corrections, will be posted to the Books / New Mexico page at Carload.com. Thanks for reading.

Acknowledgments

Writing this kind of book is like building a screen tower of bricks. So many people contributed so many pieces to the book, and my job has been to lay those bricks in place and keep the lines straight.

I want to thank everyone who helped, and I apologize in advance to anyone that I have left out of the following list. (If that's you, please remind me so I can include you in a future version.)

Thanks to

First, it sounds like pandering, but the people of New Mexico have been so friendly and helpful that I postponed another project to do this book first. Thanks to everybody I've met in the Land of Enchantment.

Joe Bob Briggs, who has been a fan of Carload.com almost since its inception. It's always great when your heroes aren't jerks.

CinemaTreasures.org, merely the best single source of information for all film theaters (including drive-ins) past and present.

Amy Schaefer at the New Mexico State Library, for finding an amazing number of newspaper clips to illuminate many of these drive-in stories.

Joan Hamblen Monninger at the Aztec Museum & Pioneer Village, for pointing me to Zang Woods' helpful 2011 booklet, *Sodas & Shows: Pop Culture in San Juan County, NM*, and discovering the origin of Spencerville.

Alane Wainwright at the New Mexico Department of Transportation, for providing historic aerial photos offering unique glimpses of some of these drive-ins.

HistoricAerials.com, an amazing resource that often shows when and where drive-ins were built.

Ivy Masterson, who passed along a few clues about Cuba's Placita Hills.

The Internet Archive, which hosts the Media History Digital Library, a huge source of theater anecdotes and occasional photos.

And of course, I need to thank my loving family for allowing and even encouraging so much effort on such a lightly regarded topic.

Graphics Notes

The front cover image was assembled by the author, with modifications, from the following ingredients:

Neon Green Light Alphabet Vector Font © Epifantsev / Depositphotos.com.
Deep space © titoOnz / Depositphotos.com.
New Mexico shield © BigAlBaloo / Depositphotos.com.
2013 photo of the Fort Union Drive-In, Las Vegas NM, by the author.

Here's a particularly important acknowledgment. Several photos were licensed through Creative Commons 3.0:
https://creativecommons.org/licenses/by/3.0/
Thanks to all of you for sharing. You can find a few dozen of my drive-in-photos with CC licensing on Flickr:
https://flickr.com/photos/carload/
Here are the CC 3.0-licensed photos in this book, in order, with URLs of their originals:

Milan Trails photo posted by Nlister at CinemaTreasures.org:
http://cinematreasures.org/theaters/48641/photos/231510
Raton 85 photo posted by dallasmovietheaters at Cinema-Treasures.org:
http://cinematreasures.org/theaters/41945/photos/80978
Taos Kit Carson photo posted by Anthony L. Vazquez-Hernandez at CinemaTreasures.org:
http://cinematreasures.org/theaters/48643/photos/288268

Index

About the Author

Michael Kilgore is the webmaster of Carload.com, a drive-in theater information source since 1998. He has been recognized for his work by the Library of Congress. Previously, he was a writer and editor for the *Kansas City Star* and other newspapers. He also wrote *Drive-Ins of Route 66* and *Drive-Ins of Colorado*.

Visit Carload.com and go to Books / New Mexico for updates, corrections, and bonus content.

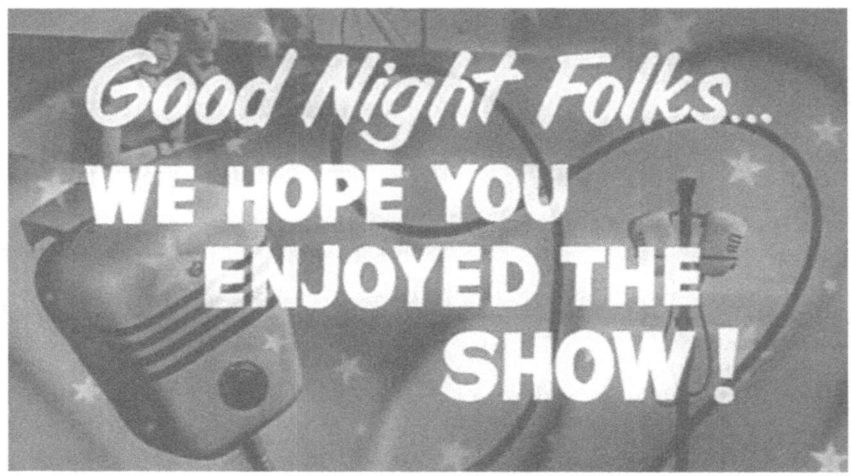